"I Do So Politely"

A Voice from the South

"*I Do So Politely*"

A Voice from the South

Robert Canzoneri

Houghton Mifflin Company · Boston
The Riverside Press · Cambridge
1965

For my father and mother

*who tried to teach us, among other
good things, that "If you really fulfill
the royal law, according to the scripture,
'You shall love your neighbor as yourself,'
you do well. But if you show partiality,
you commit sin . . ."*

Contents

"*I Do So Politely*"

A Voice from the South

I

"I Do So Politely"

In the fourth grade in Clinton, Mississippi, we were taught that

> Politeness is to do and say
> The kindest things in the kindest way.

The little rhyme jangled in my mind when I watched the televised meeting between Governor Ross Barnett of Mississippi and prospective University of Mississippi student James Meredith. It was a calm meeting; that particular encounter was for the Governor personally to bar Meredith's registration in spite of a court order. A United States Marshal went through the formality of attempting to walk through the crowd with Meredith. Gray figures on the television screen moved restlessly around the principals. James Meredith stood patiently and observed.

The Governor quoted the Tenth Amendment to the

Constitution of the United States and stated that on the basis of that Amendment he was refusing Meredith admittance to Ole Miss. Then Ross added, "I do so politely."

By some leap of memory I also associated Ross's politeness with the garden of the Devines, who lived nearby when I was a boy. Now and then in the spring a Negro boy about my age would come across the fields of sage grass to our side door and recite, "Mammy say can she have some greens and a cabbage or sump'm." We all said, and generally now say, sump'm for something. My mother would go to the garden and get a cabbage and some turnip greens and some beans and maybe some onions, and my brother and I would talk with Robert. I seem to remember playing marbles with him, too, once or twice, but although the Devines lived only a couple of hills away, we saw him only if the relief food was unpalatable or ran out.

One day when my mother brought the vegetables through the house and out the side door, she said, "Robert, don't y'all have a garden?"

"Yessum," Robert said, and then he grinned. "But it ain't got nothing in it."

The administrator of the first school I taught in had been reduced long before to the blatantly obvious. On the day of a big game I heard him say to the basketball coach, "You tell those boys if they just keep putting that ball through that hoop, they'll make a score." The least you can say for it, and the most, is that it does make sense, even if saying it doesn't. It had come, presumably, from his observation of what happens in a ball game. And it gave him something, as principal, to say.

Another of my school employers had abandoned the

flatly obvious for a more complex view of things. He used to say to the faculty and the PTA with pride evident in his voice even as he began, "It is a common saying among administrators that you can judge the discipline and morale of a school by the cleanliness of the walls of the boys' room." He reported that when he came to the school the walls of the boys' rest rooms were written all over with dirty words and had obscene pictures drawn on them. "But now," he phrased it once, "the picture has changed." The laughter that followed offended him almost as much as the obscenities on the walls.

His face would become flushed and rigid whenever on one of his frequent patrols he found a freshly scrawled item in a rest room. He would search frantically for the boy who had done it. If the guilty one could not be apprehended, the janitor was sent for. If the janitor was discreetly out of the way, he himself would angrily scrub from the walls during classes whatever visual aids had been penciled on between periods.

This same school administrator attended a campaign rally for Ross Barnett during one of Ross's unsuccessful bids for the governorship. I had just left the school, as had my Aunt Vera, who had been teaching there at the same time. Her husband was Ross's first cousin, as is my mother.

The administrator and one of my friends sat through Ross's speech, and when it was over, the administrator — a jolly man — suggested that they go meet Ross. They did. When it came their turn, Ross shook hands with my friend and then with the administrator. The administrator made conversation.

"We know Miss Vera," he said. "And we know Bob." His overture would have been cryptic enough to the

uninitiated, but it did not faze Ross. "Yes," Ross said.
"Yes." He was looking completely aside, hearing nothing,
ready for the next faceless hand to shake.

"Yes, sir," the administrator beamed. "Fine folks."

"Good to see you," Ross was saying above the next hand.

As the administrator and my friend walked away (from
the Oxford courthouse square, it was) the administrator,
bouncy as ever, said, "Very nice man. Very impressive."

My friend said, "I thought he was rude."

The administrator stopped and looked quickly around.
"Did you notice that, too?"

Ever since Bilbo, in my memory, politicians in Mississippi have been expected to give a good show in their campaign speeches. Ross would not likely have gone in at an
earlier period because what entertainment he affords is
meager and is at his own expense. One "inside" report
during his successful campaign had a committee of major
supporters going to the attending physician, as it became
evident that Ross would recover reasonably soon from
the serious injuries caused by an airplane propeller, and
asking the doctor to limit Ross's speaking severely so that
he would not talk himself out of victory.

I suspect that Ross finally won partly because of his
reputation as a highly successful lawyer. I recall a campaign movie that showed him boarding a plane for Washington to plead before the United States Supreme Court
— though that particular film may have been in the 1955
rather than the 1959 race. The man who had come through
legal entanglements and courtrooms with a good record
and plenty of money (having started out, as one of his
ardent fans told me, with shoes so thin he could stand on
a dime and tell whether it was heads or tails) was particu-

larly appealing because it was apparent that white Mississippi would need all the legal slipperiness it could exude.

I think there was another thing in his favor, in addition to his opponents, even. Ross has a fine air of polite removal from reality. His shoes have much thicker soles, now. There is some possibility that the marvelously impressive way he has of not quite making contact, apparently not quite being sure what is happening before his eyes, is what most attracted Mississippi voters: Obvious Politeness in the atmosphere of legality that surrounds the president of the bar association and pleader before the Supreme Court of the United States. The unthought, never consciously accepted motivation grew somewhere in the back of the mind: if Ross cannot, out of sheer Southern politeness or whatever, quite come to grips with the facts, he can take our side and make it legal. We vote Barnett.

The last time I saw Ross other than on television was at the 1961 Ole Miss–LSU football game. I didn't go — that is, I didn't get in. Tickets were running from $20 up at kickoff time, and so I wrote off my hour-and-a-half of wandering around the stadium as experience in sports enthusiasm, cupidity and general insanity. Near the end of the experience I heard sirens, and the crowd began to part. A Mississippi Highway Patrol car eased through, and then a large Oldsmobile with red light atop pulled in and stopped not two yards from me. A patrolman stepped quickly from the driver's seat and opened the back door, and Ross got out. The crowd was staring, and somebody said, "Howdy, Governor," and Ross said, "Hello," to the crowd.

He stood there, and I thought: Aw come on, Bob, be polite. And so I stepped forward and held out my hand

and told him my name. He shook my hand and said, "Ah
. . . yes. Yes. How's the family?" Fine, I told him, and he
reached quickly over to his left for another hand within
his politically keen peripheral vision. No hand was there,
however. His eyes wandered in the direction of the stadium.

One of the unticketed mob, standing now with necks
strained, gawking, said hungrily, "You got a ticket, Governor?"

Ross had turned to go, but he turned back. "Yes. Yes,"
he said politely. "Thank you, but I do have one."

The man spoke with some disgust. "I mean an extra
one. For me."

"Oh," Ross said vaguely. "Oh. No, I'm afraid not."
He was in Louisiana, and it might be that these folks
couldn't vote for him, but he was polite anyway. "I wish
I did have an extra one," he said, moving away. "I would
give it to . . ." he was scanning the starved faces with some
comprehension now, ". . . to somebody."

Back before the vacillation prior to and on the day of
the Ole Miss riot, Ross Barnett's inability to see what he
was looking at and keep his attention upon it seemed
funny. One fine story, at least largely contrived, came
out of the early campaigning days.

According to the story, Shine Morgan of Oxford was
Ross's campaign manager in North Mississippi, and one
day he took Ross on a swift speaking tour of half a dozen
towns. While Ross was speaking to the crowd that would
gather on the street, Shine would single out the most important people and line them up for Ross to shake hands
with particularly. After the speech, Ross would come
down the line, look uncomprehendingly at each man,
shake hands heartily, and say, "Ah . . . can't call the name.
Recognize the face, though. Knew your daddy!" The

man would tell his name, and Ross would say, "Yes. Yes. Why sure," and already be moving to the next one. "Ah . . . can't call the name . . ."

By the time he would get through the line to where Shine was, Ross would be completely glazed. He would come right on with that benign lift of the sides of the face and that groping eye; he would grab Shine's hand and say, "Ah . . . can't call the name. Recollect the face." And Shine would whisper at him fiercely, "I'm Shine Morgan, your campaign manager. Come on."

They would take off for the next town, Ross would speak, Shine would line them up, Ross would fumble down the line, and finally there would be the grabbing of Shine's hand again. "Ah . . . can't call the name . . ." And Shine would pull him away, saying, "I'm Shine Morgan, your campaign manager." This went on through four of the towns, and finally in the fifth Ross came down the line again, repeating his formula. He released the last man and grabbed Shine's hand again. "Can't call the name offhand," he said. "Know the face."

"I'm Shine Morgan, your campaign manager," Shine said. "But I'll be damned if I'll vote for you."

However fictitious the particular story, it obviously grew from a seed of truth. Is it any wonder that Ross Barnett could stand envisioning in his legal mind the Constitution of the United States with a gap for the Fourteenth Amendment? Is it any wonder that he could stand there quoting the Tenth Amendment — "The powers not delegated to the United States by the constitution nor prohibited by it to the States, are reserved to the States respectively, or to the people" — as if the phrase "or to the people" were not there although he was saying it? Is it any wonder that he could stand there with James Meredith not only in the abstract a citizen of the state, but in

actual flesh a man, facing him? Is it any real wonder that
Ross should be the chosen one to say, "I do so politely"?

It was for this that a majority of the people of the state
of Mississippi with voting privileges elected him governor.

Senator John F. Kennedy was only a rumored possibility
for the Democratic Presidential nomination when he spoke
in the Victory room of the Heidelberg Hotel in Jackson,
Mississippi, at a meeting sponsored by the Young Democrats, but he was that possibility in everyone's mind. The
Republican chairman had issued a challenge to the Massa-
chusetts Senator to explain his stand — in Mississippi —
on the Supreme Court integration decision of 1954.

The large crowd obviously liked the young Senator,
and when he mentioned the challenge and responded to
it with an unequivocal statement, the audience was dis-
posed in his favor. He said that he believed the Supreme
Court decision to represent the law of the land which
must be obeyed. Then he challenged the Republican
chairman to explain his stand on (as I now recall it)
Richard Milhouse Nixon, and got a delighted ovation.

Afterward, in the men's room, I was waiting my turn
behind two old men. One said to the other, "Well, what
did you think of the boy?"

"Makes a good speech," the other replied.

"Did mighty well, I thought."

"You know," the second one said, " he just might be our
next President."

"Wouldn't be surprised," the first said. He was silent
for a moment, and then he added, "What he said there
about that Supreme Court decision, of course, now, he
had to say that. I don't really think he means it."

"Naw." The other nodded wisely. "He had to say that."

II

After the Surrender

WE SOUTHERN white people have lived side by side, back door to back door with the Negro for all these many years, but we do not really know who he is or what he thinks.

It is difficult enough to put into words what "we" are like within any given community, even though we may be perfectly at home there, share the general attitudes, and be confident that our behavior in any situation will be acceptable. But it is impossible to convey what an essentially alien group is like, a community which has operated — must operate — in secret, so far as "we" are concerned. A sociologist may be able to catalogue various aspects of a society foreign to him, but such an attempt always calls to mind Mark Twain's reply to his wife when, to shame him, she repeated his outburst of profanity; like Livy, they may know the words, but I suspect they really don't at all have the tune.

Probably the best I can do is to record a fragment of the
tune as I have overheard it from some distance.

The distance itself has varied, though much less than
many white people in Mississippi like to think. One kind
of tacit separation between the races existed until about
the end of World War II. Then began a relative relaxation
of the boundaries for a period which lasted until the Supreme Court decision of 1954 to desegregate the schools.
The relaxation was, in my experience, largely on the part
of veterans on the GI Bill who were bold enough to exer-
cise the traditional student prerogative of inquiry into the
assumptions of the previous generation. In retrospect that
time seems to some Southerners one in which we were
moving in the right direction, and they believe that if we
had not been pushed from "outside," so that reaction developed, we would have "solved our own problems." No
one has ever gone on to indicate where it was we were
headed or what the solution would have been. Integration? A chummy sort of segregation? Or simply the status
quo established — with no outside interference? I have
grave reservations about "the relaxed period," but for the
sake of division, and because it seems to me there was at
least a superficial change during those years, I will separate my own experiences into the three periods of time:
prior to World War II, from then until 1954, and since.

My first recollections of a Negro are of a man born, as I
remember his account in getting my mother to calculate
his age, three years after the surrender. I suspect the surrender he meant was that of Vicksburg rather than Appo-
mattox. His name was Bob Eubanks. He lived in a very
small house of weathered boards; I seem to remember
newspapers on the inside walls, to keep out the wind, but
that may be from another house or even from a book. In
the same way, I seem to recall a washpot on the bare clay

in front of the house, and the smell of burnt-out fires. I believe he was married and had children, though I also believe his wife had died and the children were away by the time I was any size.

We could get to Old Bob's house (we called him that to distinguish him from me) by crossing the pasture downhill to the west, turning at the big hickory tree at the foot of which we used to crack the thick-hulled nuts between brickbats, and walking on southward through brush and a field to where the house stood alone, well off the highway that ran in front of our house and curved toward his. We seldom went to his house; he came up the hill fairly often to ours.

He had a mule, and he plowed our garden every spring. Sometimes, when we were little, he would put us up on the sharp ridge of the mule's back and let us ride while he plowed. One of our neighbors commented that Bob and his mule were so slow you had to line them up with a tree to be sure they were moving.

When he worked for us — plowing, hauling things in his wagon, killing a dog with black-tongue, fixing the pasture fence — he would take his meals in our kitchen, where we always ate except for special company. But he ate after we had eaten. Sometimes he spoke in enigmatic figures, as when he told my mother, indicating his coffee cup, "This foot ain't got no sock on it." My mother and father did not use sugar in their coffee, and she had forgotten to offer the sugar to Bob.

When Old Bob had finished some small job, he would come to the back door to report.

"How much do I owe you, Bob?" My mother would say.

"Whatever you say, Mrs. Canzoneri." (Mi' Can-neh, he would call it.)

Each would try to get the other to decide, and finally

one of them would say, "Is fifteen cents all right?" It was
during the depression.

The other would say, "If that's all right with you."

Then, more often than not Old Bob would hold up his
hand and say, "Just leave it in the bank, Mi' Can-neh."
She would write down the amount, and on some later day
Bob would come to the back door, on the way to the little
store a mile down the highway, and get some tobacco
money — a nickel, maybe — out of the bank.

We all were fond of Old Bob, yet a racial separation
did exist. It would, I am reasonably sure, have been uncomfortable for him if we had crossed it — perhaps viola-
tion would have been impossible for him. The separation
had been as much a part of his existence as the house and
the hickory tree and the mule, and it had been drilled into
us (in my case not as teaching at home) along with morals
and memory verses.

Of course, Bob was not prevented from making judg-
ments on his white neighbors. A new family moved out
into "the country" from Jackson, and the woman dressed
always as if she were four feet from the next house and
would be on a sidewalk if she stepped out the front door.
With lipstick, too, which in those parts at that time many
women her age never wore at all.

"She's all right," Bob told us. "All she need is a few
more twists."

Of another neighboring woman he reported, "She's as
good a woman as ever wore a shoe."

When I was very small — about the time I was in the
first of Southern Baptist missionary organizations, the
Sunbeams, and, having misunderstood the word "tither,"
was singing away each Monday afternoon "Jesus wants
me for a tiger" — I rode one day with Old Bob in his

wagon to get some hay. We sat on a gray, weather-scored plank set across the wagon bed, jolting behind the mule. Bob's hands were dry and gray-black on the slack reins. I asked him if he knew the song "Jesus Loves Me." He said he knew one something like that, and told me the first lines. I had never heard of it. He tried another. I had never heard of that one either. And so he said he must not know that song.

I could not imagine anyone's not knowing "Jesus Loves Me." One might as easily not know how to talk, or how to breathe.

(An account was around during his administration about a speech Ross Barnett made at a synagogue in which he referred more than once to the congregation as fine Christian people. When Ross sat down the rabbi remarked that it wasn't often his people were called fine Christians. According to the account, someone explained it to Ross, whereupon he said, "Oh. Well, I'm sure you're all fine Christians at heart.")

As Old Bob got older, some neighbors took him in, the woman who was as good as any who ever wore a shoe, and fixed him a room in the basement of their house. I remember the room as pleasant with white walls, Old Bob seated on the bed, a Bible nearby. I think he had on glasses, then. When our neighbors moved, he went with them.

He and my father had always been friends, I suppose. I remember an incident when Dad had an operation and was home from the hospital all stitched up so that it hurt to laugh. My grandmother was here (the Mississippi one, I never knew the Sicilian one), and Old Bob came up to see Dad. We all stood around; it was an event. A discussion of age came up, and it was determined that Bob was somewhat above seventy, as I remember. "I may be getting old," he said, "but if I had somebody to clap for me, I could still cut a pigeon-wing."

My grandmother, as interesting a person as ever lived, said she used to clap for dances, years ago, and so she started clapping, and Old Bob did a little dance, a very nimble one.

What set Dad to laughing, though, was my grandmother's reaction. She looked very solemn, when the dance was over. "That's the first time I have clapped for a dance in forty years," she said. "The Lord forgive me."

It was several years later, after the neighbors had moved to another town and we had moved to Kentucky, that Dad was in Mississippi on a trip, and he went to see Old Bob for the last time. They looked at each other and Dad said, "Bob, I'm so glad to see you I could hug your neck." And Bob said, "Why don't you?" The two men put their arms about each other and cried.

At some time in my early childhood a very bulky Negro woman took care of us, perhaps while my mother was having my younger brother. Out of that unremembered past we retained her promise that she would take us fishing, and so every time for years that we saw her, we would say, "When you going to take us fishing?" and she would laugh and say, "Oh, 'bout next Tuesday."

I don't know where this particular family lived when the fishing promise took place, but later on they had a small house on the back of our neighbor's place. Several hundred yards behind our house the railroad ran through a deep cut, eroded on our side into grown-over gullies which were gradually being filled with rusting cans and junk. Their house was rather near the railroad. It was apparently a relatively solid house, much newer and more upright and tighter than Old Bob's. The wood was unpainted, but it still retained its color as long as I remember noticing it. I seem to recall a tin roof, or some tin on the roof.

The wife did the housework for our white neighbors. She was so big that when she had an emergency appendectomy, the doctor had to cut through nine inches of fat. At least that was the figure that stuck in my mind from the account of her employer as told to somebody who told it to somebody who didn't tell it to me, but did tell it in my hearing. Her husband, who did the outside chores, was small and very strong and had the reputation of being reliable.

I heard the two of them talking once about a Negro nightclub a mile or two away that flourished for some time so loudly that we could hear it on still nights, and I remember my feeling of awe. It was a world completely separate from mine. Of course, I knew nothing about the white nightclubs, either, although one was virtually in sight down the highway from us (its name, part of the time, was Idle Hours, and Old Bob used to call it Idle Wires). But the Negro nightclub was forever closed to me, even assuming I should one day have the audacity to walk into any kind of nightclub; and they had actually been there.

They had children, but of them I remember only one clearly. He was a boy about my age, and he was in his early teens when a couple of incidents occurred that left an impression. One was his helping us dig out a septic tank, and his high spirits. He danced around and sang and acted a monkey for us, and we thought he was hilarious. We also thought it was funny that whenever he was asked his real name (he went by a nickname), he stuck the "Junior" in as middle name, as in John Junior Smith. He told us once that he was a member of a particular church a couple of miles toward Jackson, but that he was thinking of resigning. A member of our church couldn't resign, and so of course we thought the whole idea funny and primitive.

The other thing I remember about him was that he got a job on a truck, a milk delivery truck, I think it was, and fell off the back and split his head open so that they had to take quite a number of stitches (fifteen or nineteen, or maybe it was nine inches of fat. When I was young things had a way of being what they weren't, exactly. I remember telling one of my grade school teachers that my grandfather from Sicily had come to Jackson but wouldn't come on out to see us, only seven or eight miles from downtown, and then realizing some year or so later that it had been New York he had come to, and I'm not sure where the "wouldn't come on down to see us" came from. The realization gave me an uncomfortable feeling of having been naïve and provincial in the extreme; it was an exceptionally accurate feeling). Anyway, his head had been severely hurt, and it was said that if he had not been a Negro, i.e., hardheaded and thick of skull, he would have been killed.

We lived just between Jackson and the small college town of Clinton. Going toward Clinton on what was then U.S. 80, a two-lane blacktop road, we would go around an S curve, the middle of which was a narrow underpass where the railroad came out of the cut and over the highway — and we loved to ride under just as a train would "run over" us. As we rounded the last of the S curve, we could see Old Bob's house off to the left. Then there was a gravel road off the same direction, and some distance along it, out of sight of the highway, was the shack of the Devines. Another shack was near the road-side up a bank, so that it seemed to be silhouetted against the sky. If I recall correctly, it is gone now; it gradually deteriorated so that not even the poorest Negro could live in it. I suspect that there was no work to be done, finally, for whoever owned the pasture land it was on. Or perhaps pasture land was only the last site of the rotting house, and once, when it was newer and more or less habitable, it had been surrounded by cotton planted up close to the door. When I think of it that way it seems true, but then I have seen so many such houses in so many fields of cotton that I may be transplanting that one so as to make coherent the factors of decay.

At one time a short, heavy-shouldered Negro man lived in the house. We knew him by name, and it seems vaguely that he may have done some odd job or other for us when Old Bob wasn't available. I did know him very well by sight, and used to see him pass along the shoulder of the highway in front of our house, apparently going to the little store for some tobacco or something. I say I did know him by sight, because my brother once accused me, as we stood looking at another Negro walking along that highway, of not being able to tell one Negro from an-other. It was often true, and his indignation was justified.

But this man I knew, and I have a picture still of him walking toward his house in his same drab work clothes, carrying a suitcase for the tall smartly dressed yellow girl who sauntered along behind. And then perhaps a day or so later we saw them coming in the opposite direction, possibly back to the bus stop at the little store, and as they passed she jumped up onto him and he carried her piggyback along the highway, trudging with the suitcase.

Toward Jackson from us the Negro houses were all away from the highway, and my recollection of Negroes in that

direction centers at a couple of small stores. I waited for
my mother outside one, as a small boy, and watched some
Negro women dipping snuff in a nearby car. One rolled
down the window beside her to spit, but she failed to
roll it down far enough.

Such sights as that, plus the obvious fact of the poor
houses and clothes, the lack of education, and the apparent immorality (immorality = sex and whiskey and
crap shooting) of the Negroes around us, made most of
our neighbors and to a degree ourselves a bit queasy about
their cleanliness at times. Later, when we lived in Kentucky, where there were very few Negroes, some white
families took over this function; one family down the
street from us found the outhouse too cold in winter and
so chopped a hole in the living room floor.

It was true, too, that the blank caution of the Negro
could sometimes ruin our fun. In grade school we used
to ask the unsuspecting, so long as unsuspecting people
were still around, such questions as, "Are you a cow?" And
when they would reply in the negative, we would respond,
"Don't worry little calf, you'll grow up." We wore it out
on all of our contemporaries, and so one day we tried it
on the Negro janitor. He was a large man, or seemed so
to us, and always mild and genial. It was around at the
back of the grade school building, where the concrete
steps led down to the outside entrance to the boys' basement, as the rest room was always called, and we would
wrap ourselves around the hollow black metal railings as
we tried to catch the janitor out.

"Are you a cow?" we would ask him.

"I's whatever you says I is." Politely.

"Well, are you a horse?"

"I's whatever you says I is."

"Aw, come on. You're supposed to *say!* Are you a dog?"

"I's whatever you says I is."

It's the only time I can remember being dissatisfied with his work as janitor.

When I was just big enough to help get hay for our two cows, I heard a young Negro's humorous speculations about doomsday.

It was extremely hot, and we had stopped pitching hay onto the wagon to go under a tree for a drink of water — my brothers and I and two young Negro men. They were the bosses; they knew the job. The tree stood alone on a hill from which the thick grass had been cut, and a large cemetery spread out beneath us.

"See that part down yonder with the new grave dug in it?" one of the Negroes said. "They just opened up that section last year. It's all right now, dry like this, but that dirt is pure dee ole clay, and when it gets wet — look out! Last spring we dug a grave down yonder for ole man Smith in Jackson, and it come a rain and wet that clay, and we cover him up in that wet clay and pack it down, and it dry out harder'n any concrete."

He paused and pointed far down the hill and across the rolling, well-kept lawn of graves to the new lower section. "Why, man," he said, and laughed. "Why, man, when Gabriel blow his trumpet, ole man Smith ain't going to be able to get up from where he is through that hard clay. He going to have to tunnel clean under this hill to get out!"

The Negro was in his place; nobody had to say so, everybody knew it, accepted it. What we didn't realize then was that on the day of judgment he would have to tunnel clean under the next hill to get out.

III

Before Judgment Day

ONE EVENING in 1948 a friend and I went into a small store on the outskirts of a small Mississippi town. The store, open later than the larger stores, made its money mostly on the bread and milk people forgot to buy from their regular grocers, and from the beer it could sell, being just beyond the city limits of a dry town. A car pulled up to the gas pumps outside, and two white men got out of the front seat, a Negro man out of the back. The two white men came in the front door and stood talking with the grocer, but the Negro man went around to the back of the store. Apparently there was a beer-drinking room for the Negroes back there, because in a moment the man's head appeared in an opening and he asked for a beer. The grocer took a bottle from the cooler and took the Negro man's money, and the face disappeared. In a moment, however, the Negro man came into the front

part of the store. He was an aging man in a dark suit
with a dark hat and with skin of a very dark, rich color.
His face was a marvel of plasticity.

"Yassuh, boss," the Negro said. He was playing with
debasement; there was riotous good humor, real or assumed, just beneath the mobile features. He had fastened
his eyes on my friend and came gliding over to him. "I
says to myself just now, I says, that young man there, he
going to buy this here old man a bottle of beer. I says
to myself, now I can tell by looking at him that he got a
kind heart, yassuh, and he ain't going to let this old fellow
quit with just one beer when he thirsty, no suh. He a
generous young man, I says."

He stood in a pleading, elastic crouch in the dark suit,
waiting, openly playing the game. My friend laughed
and said, "All right, you win," and handed him some
money.

The Negro said, "Didn't I say so? A fine young man.
Tell it by looking at him, I says." He gave the money to
the grocer and got his beer. He did not return to the
back room, although obviously only white people drank
out front, but stood with the beer in his hand and raised
it in the dim light of the store; the dark amber bottle
gurgled into the black face.

"Yassuh," he said after a moment. He assumed a
crouch, the crouch of the evangelist, now, and his face
came alive with the good news. "Don't it say in the
Scripture, right there in the book of Acts, in the twentieth
chapter and the thirty-fifth verse, 'It is more blessed to
give than to receive'?" His arm went up in a ministerial
gesture, half mocking but full of energy. The white men
all smiled indulgently. He was putting on a show. It was
like having the shoeshine boy call attention to himself,

doing a little dance to excuse being out of his place, so that he would really be in it and everybody could enjoy the show and feel generous. "Yassuh, and don't the Lord say right there in the book of Matthew the fifth chapter and the forty-second verse, 'Give to him that asketh thee,' because it's good to give! It's good to give." He straightened and looked around him with wide innocent eyes at the grocer and the two white men.

"Yassuh, the Scripture calls for it, and I knows the Scripture." He held up one hand suddenly, calling the throngs to silence. "And then they's history. Look back into the beginnings of this country. Back yonder in fo'teen hundred and ninety-two ole Columbus come sailing across to the island of San Salvador and found this whole new world. And it wasn't till sixteen and seven — sixteen and seven that Captain John Smith and all them folks settled there in Jamestown in Virginia, and them that wouldn't work wasn't allowed to eat." He was acting it out, that black face working with every shading of his voice. And now he stopped dead still. No one moved.

"Sixteen and nineteen," he said. "Sixteen and nineteen. That's when the first ones of my people come to this land. Sixteen and nineteen. Yassuh." He swung into action again, in that athletic crouch, his arm extended, hailing the ships that came into Jamestown. "They brought them in by the shipload as slaves, and they sold them for tobacco." He paused and held the scene there a silent moment, and then he repeated softly, "Sold them for tobacco."

I could hear the silence. It was stunned, tense. Surely he would not complain, right here in front of us white folks. He wouldn't dare!

But the Negro went on. His face was tragic now. "Sold them for tobacco." He looked around at us all, no longer the preacher and no longer the historian and no longer, it seemed, the performer, but just himself, a lone black man whose fathers had been sold for tobacco. "You think that's going to make me mad? You think that's going to make this ole black man mad cause they took my people and sold them for tobacco? You think that's going to make me mad and I'm not going to chew any more tobacco?" His face lit up, and he threw himself into the evangelistic stance again. "Naw suh!" he shouted. "I going to chew all the tobacco I wants to!"

He carried it off, about as beautifully as I have ever seen anything carried off. But he had to know just how far to press, just when to dissolve into the clever fool.

Once in a while I have been conscious of a glimpse into a strange world all around and all throughout my own, as if with something like infrared glasses I could see the whole living structure. It is almost, for an occasional moment, as if I could see the wind and the whole world of air. But there has been nothing in me that would hold the view long enough; there has been none of the proper substance in me to make it possible for me really to exist in that world, even to visit it as Alice did Looking Glass House.

One glimpse came in the casual remark of old Uncle Tim. I had seldom called a Negro man Uncle. We referred to Old Bob as Old. Not as Mr. Eubanks; that was never done. But many white people called a Negro man Uncle if he were due respect within the range of possibility for respect that a Negro had. The respect was genuine, it was just damnably limited. In my home we avoided the Uncle habit, and I think it must have been the result of a kind of embarrassment in using it. I don't know. Anyway, I learned Uncle Tim through another family, and that's the way he was introduced to me.

He started in immediately telling me about himself. He was rather tall and striking, erect, very old. He spoke in short, sedate phrases: "Member of the church," he said. "Sings in the choir. Second tenor. Sings solos. Has to muffle my voice when I sings with the choir. Too strong for 'em." For a moment there was life in the church I had passed almost every day of my life.

I met Uncle Tim right after World War II, when I returned to college. There was talk of trying to bridge some gaps between the races, then. Where are those bright young men now? I know about a few, and maybe they were the only ones who really wanted to try anyway, and none of us knew how. We had Uncle Tim sing some Negro spirituals for one of our literature classes, and we loved it and so did he. But he was of another age, and even we knew he was as we sat there in the basement of the slave-built Historic Old Chapel, which had according to legend served the Union forces as hospital and stable, and heard the ancient voice working in the old style around and beyond the tune. I can see him, now, straight and unabashed before the college class, his dark brown eyelids tightly closed, singing about going home to Jesus.

Earlier, before I went off to war, I had known a Negro man who worked at a cleaning shop downtown. I consider myself his friend to this day, and see him when I go back to the town. He has always known His Place and has kept it. Although he and my father were acquainted when my father was in school there, I knew only his first name until recent years, and still he calls me Mr. Bob.

Some younger Negroes could, and did, get by with what would now be called impertinence given the right people and circumstances. One of these was a little black carhop everybody called Snowball. We used to drive out to the cafe at all hours of the day and night, and so Snowball knew us well enough. One day a friend of mine was driving into the gravel parking area too fast. He put on the brakes rather showily and slid to a stop just outside the small house window in the front of the frame building. Snowball got up slowly, sauntered over to the car, and asked casually, "You want me to raise the window so you can go on in?"

I worked on a weekly newspaper for one hot summer. It was on a Negro street, between the Elite Cafe and a cleaning shop. We used to telephone the Negro cafe next door and ask them to bring us Cokes. They would answer the phone, "E-light Cafe." The cleaning shop was a very good one and was patronized by Negroes and white people alike.

One day as I came up the street by the cleaning shop, toward the courthouse square, a pair of Negro children spoke to me. They were under school age and had that incredible brightness most children lose in the early grades of school. They were dressed very neatly, as if it were Sunday, and their freshly bathed skin was the color of creamed coffee. Both of them spoke, the boy and the girl, and so I stopped and said, "Hello."

The little boy looked up at me, grinning. "You know me?"

"Sure," I lied. "Of course I know you."

He said, "What my name?"

On the newspaper there was a young Negro linotypist, an excellent one. Nearly always his work was flawless, but once in setting up an ad for me, he badly misspelled several words. I handed it back to him and said, "What happened here?"

He took one look at it and laughed. "I spelled it the way I says it and not the way I spells it."

He had a fine sense of humor and an interesting way of seeing things. One day I went to the Oldsmobile place to pick up an ad and bought an old Cadillac. It started a trend. The printer went down and bought an Oldsmobile convertible, and then the Negro linotypist went down and bought a secondhand Olds. He was crazy about it, and all he could talk about all day was his new car. Finally he decided what he was going to do. "This weekend," he said, "I'm going to get in that car and fill it up with gas and drive till the gauge say half full and turn around and drive back home."

Several days later, he began to have a kind of inexplicable trouble I have often had too: every so often he would step wrong somehow and kick his anklebone. Once you do that, you're doomed to do it for some unknown number of times until for no reason the curse is lifted. Anyway, during one whole morning he would exclaim "Ouch!" every now and then as he walked to the stockroom or back to his linotype machine. Again in a few minutes we would hear him complain. "Keep kicking my ankles," he told us, one trip, and then on the way back he said, "I guess my feet done forgot how to walk, been driving that car so much."

The barriers may have been nudged, prior to 1954, but not significantly. So far as I can recall no real dents were made. I do remember a lot of white bull sessions and some things in our college publications that might get a man denounced today — but it doesn't take much to

get a man denounced today. And I do remember a Negro
college graduate who gave a friend and me a ride, one
day, and our trying to talk to him about the whole
situation. But he was older by a few years than we, and
we got the impression that he felt mostly superior and
indulgent, and that he was right.

During part of this period of mutual understanding (as
the entrenched Mississippian now likes to consider it, looking back with grave tolerance upon his formerly tolerant
self) we lived in Oxford, where white life went along
smoothly in ignorance of the Negro world around it. Except that going out from the campus toward Batesville we
had to drive along beside a few unpainted shacks, just to
remind us. And farther out, off the highway, I knew, if
I thought of it, where a Negro mechanic lived with his
family. I knew about him because he had taken the
remnants of my old Cadillac, whose block had been
treacherously cracked by an unseasonable drop to five
degrees over Thanksgiving while we were in Kentucky
and it wasn't. With no money to buy a new block, and
little money to be had for the car as junk, I had let it go
to the Negro mechanic on his promise of payment as car
if he could fix the block and of payment as junk if he
couldn't. He got it running briefly — I saw him and some
of his family in it — and so after a few days, when no
news came, I went out to ask about it. I saw him again
only by leaving a threat with an informant.

I would go to his house and he would always be somewhere else, nobody knew quite where. I tried to tell
them that I was merely trying to find out what the situation was, but still, although I would make a sort of ap-
pointment, he would always be — elsewhere. Finally
I said that I would have to get the sheriff to find him,

and so he came to see me. The car was not really fixed. One of his children had died. He was broke. He wanted to try some more to fix the car. He would pay me some on it the next week and then some more in a couple of weeks when he got a check from some man, named but unknown to me. Of course, I said. I just didn't like to make a deal and not be able to find out what was going on. I never saw him again, and of course I didn't go looking. But I knew where he lived in a little weathered unpainted shack up a bank from the gravel road, where a young Negro woman or a child would come to the gaping doorway and say, "He not here. Naw suh, I don't rightly know just where he'd be right now. Yes suh, he meant to be here, but now he having to work late and all . . . Naw suh, he not at work now. I don't rightly know where he'd be right at this minute." I suppose he lived there. They seemed to think he did at all times except right at this minute.

It was in Oxford, too, that I became aware of Blind Jim. Blind Jim was an Ole Miss institution. At pep rallies and at football games he would be placed in a strategic position to cheer the Rebels wildly onward, waving his Confederate flag. Then he would work his way through the crowd or up through the stadium, hat in hand, for the wages of his minstrelry. Poor old gray-haired Negro man, a willing sort of blind slave to condescending students and their cast-off money. I was always embarrassed to look him in the face, even though he could not see me.

Driving near Jackson one day, I stopped for a large, elderly Negro man and opened the front door for him to get in beside me. He did, and we talked. He never did bring the race problem into the open, but he managed to talk about it unmistakably. I tried to talk in his terms, and I believe I conveyed to him the idea that perhaps things were getting better; but he did not respond with any hope. "Nothing's done any good," he said. "We've tried and nothing's done any good. It looks like the only thing left to do is pray, and that's not going to help either."

IV

Another World

My own realization of the extent of racial separation in the South was intensified not long before the Supreme Court decision awoke us all to it and spurred on a rabid defense of it. I was aroused about three one morning by the siren of a fire engine as it screamed past my window. The town was small, and fires were not very common. Perhaps I would have gone back to sleep anyway, but the fire truck stopped as soon as it got past our place, it seemed, and I lay there for a moment realizing that fires sometimes happen to people we know.

The people I knew in that town, for the most part, I liked. Many of them had gone out of their way to be good to us. My landlord and his wife did everything to make us comfortable and to help out in any sort of emergency. I was teaching in the high school at the current meager salary rate, but the superintendent always tried to see to it that I found some way to make enough money outside to supplement the salary when necessary. The newspaper editor and his wife did the same. Christmastime when we were planning a trip to visit my parents in Kentucky, one man became so concerned about the prospect of our taking so long a trip in the old car I had that he insisted we take his new expensive car and charge to him any repairs or whatever became necessary on the road. We didn't, but the town was good to us.

And so, in spite of my habit of avoiding fires, wrecks, and all unpleasantness, I got out of bed and went to the window. The flames were very bright in the dark night, and seemed to be just beyond my landlord's roof, next door. I could not tell whose house it was, but it was frighteningly near. I dressed hurriedly and went out.

When I reached the street it was obvious that the fire was not quite so close as I had thought, but still it was extremely bright and apparently nearby. I could hear, or thought I could hear, the flames. I hurried down the street, walking. A car or two passed going toward the fire.

A few houses down I came to the railroad, and still the fire seemed about the same distance from me as it had seemed from the beginning. Flames leapt high into the darkness, and there was a hungry roar. I walked on. Beyond the railroad there were a few houses along the street I lived on, and then there were some warehouses and such, and then country, so far as I could remember.

A long block past the railroad, I came to the fire truck. Some volunteer firemen were trying to get the hose hooked onto a fire hydrant — the closest one to the burning house, I gathered, although I still could not locate the house exactly. I turned off the main road to the right,

and I walked for a short block or two on an unpaved
street between Negro houses in an area I had never
noticed before. Orange-red flames lighted small frame
houses. Some had small porches with spindling banisters;
some had little yards with small picket fences and with
beds of flowers in the corners of bare dirt yards.

I had to turn off that street onto a lesser one to approach, at last, the burning house. The fire was on the
left-hand side of the dirt street beyond a vacant lot. As I
walked in the street toward the high flames, a group of
Negro children moved slowly toward the fire through the
vacant lot from some houses beyond. The children ranged
from twelve or fourteen down. As the older ones, all
girls, got rather close to the house they screamed and ran
back, with all the little ones in a rush about them. I
thought it was simply the intense heat that had forced
them back.

The heat was terrible. The little house had apparently
been made of pitch pine, and it was burning like a torch.
Most of the structure was gone, but from the heavy beams,
which were exposed just above the ground, arose a skeleton of two-by-fours, mostly charred like burnt match-
stems. Nearby a creosoted utility pole was sizzling and
flaming up the near side. The hose would not reach.

A volunteer fireman was standing in the road, apparently to be of some help when some help should become
possible, if ever. None became possible. The house was
gone. No others were quite close enough to catch. A mob
of people crowded the road in front of the house and as
far into what had been the yard as the heat would allow.
With the walls and roof and most of the skeleton gone, the
heat was apparently less forbidding than it had been for
a few moments. I worked my way up to the front of the
group. Since I was there, I would see it.

Then I saw why the children had screamed and run. On the floor of a front room — or on the dirt where the floor had been — lay the charred corpse of a Negro man. I assumed he was a Negro. He was charred black like the burnt wood, and he lay there in awkward angularity, as if caught in a running attempt to reach out for the sill of the next room. In the next room, only a few feet away, lay another charred corpse. It was not so easily visible, because the heavy beam athwart the house was burning between me and it. The house had been very small. The first corpse seemed to stretch out across the entire width of the front room. There had been, it appeared, only four such rooms.

The flames still played around the two dead men, and the heat and smoke were still forbidding. Negro men were standing in silent rows, watching. Finally behind me I heard a couple of them talking. "Who is it?" one of them said. "It's old Soandso," the other said. "And while it's still burning we ought to go and get old Whatsisname and throw that son of a bitch in too."

I moved over to the other bank of people, on the right. A white man, very nearly obese, and a tall white woman were talking, off from the crowd a few feet. It began to appear that both of them owned houses in this Negro section, and that they had come down to check on their property. The house belonged to the woman, I gathered, and apparently she had something like $2500 in insurance on that and another house or some other houses. They talked insurance for a moment.

The woman said that she thought that the man in the front part of the house was the renter, a no-account sort who used the front as a sort of cafe and lived in the back. He was no loss. Worthless. The other man, she thought, was a Negro man in from the country, the father of nine children. He and his wife had had an argument, and he had come into town to spend the night. He had been sleeping on a cot in the back room when the fire started, and apparently he had never waked up.

A young Negro man in the very clean gray uniform of a local car dealer was standing nearby with a cheap orange rain hat in his hand. Such hats were a sort of fad, then. They were very bright, very shiny; they almost shone in the dark. The local ten cent stores carried them for something less than a dollar. The young man said that he had discovered the fire. It was already going strong when he saw it, and he came to the house to arouse the people and see what could be done. He said the man in front had been running around in the room, passing the door, apparently in a panic. The young man said that he had tried to get him to come out the door, but he kept running around frantically. The heat and smoke were so strong already that they drove the young man back when he tried to go in after the man. Finally he stood gasping in the doorway and tried to grab the man as he came past, but all he got was that orange hat. Then he had to leave, and he went and called the fire department.

He stood there with the hat, showing it. It was shiny and new looking. So far as I could see it was not in the slightest marred by smoke or flame.

The lines of Negroes shifted from time to time. Some men would come up and look in for a few minutes, and then they would move back and others would be there. Often it was quiet, but sometimes there was laughter, and an occasional white man came over and looked and asked his quiet questions and looked again. The fire burned itself on down. I went home, past the fire engine whose hose would not reach from the nearest fire hydrant.

My clothes smelled of pine smoke and of death and of that other world just beyond the railroad tracks and just off the main street. I could not bear the smell of smoke for some time. I was never in the Negro community again. It was too foreign, too strange, too separate.

Afterward, we lived in Oxford again, and then in a small town in Alabama in the Black Belt, so called originally because of the belt of black soil through there, although local citizens often explained the label as resulting from the dense population of Negroes, who had been brought there as slaves because of the rich black soil. The white hub of the town was surrounded by a wide wheel of Negroes. Behind our set of houses were a fence, a few trees, and Negro houses on a street that did not connect directly with ours.

We got to know, in the few months we were there, only one Negro. She was an elderly woman of some real gentility; she lived in a rather nice house with a solid porch and many flowers. Her living room was straight lower income middle class, with its photographs of her children who had gone to college in the North and lived there now. She took care of our children for us a few times, and they were very fond of her, as were we.

The street in front of her house was not safe for an automobile, and I would park the car and walk a couple of houses down to knock on her door rather than honk the horn for her. But she was the only Negro we knew there, and that tenuously.

After a couple of years outside the South, in Kentucky (the Southern Fried Chicken signs across the river from Cincinnati used to put me in convulsions, that area was so un-Southern, I thought), we returned to Mississippi to

notice at once a significant change in the vocabulary of
the Negroes. The word "citizen" had been added. Never
before had I heard a Negro use it — certainly not in speaking of another Negro. But now I began to hear it from
Negroes speaking to me about one another: "Yessuh, he's
a good citizen."

But my status now as "Professor" had removed me even
further from the world of the relatively uneducated, and
that included most of the Negroes. I was surprised once
to hear that a Negro woman who was recommending a
replacement for herself, to do housework, made the point
quite clearly that though the replacement was fine, she
did live on the other side of the tracks. It reminded me
that the Negro people, of course, had their own separate
society, a fact I had been most aware of some years before
at the fire.

In a little Alabama town I had an interesting experience
with some elderly Negroes of the older variety, untouched,
it seemed, by the new movements and the new ideas.
My brother-in-law asked me to drive an old Negro man
to his home with some groceries. Normally Bill drove him,
when he came to the store with his pension check and
cashed it and stocked up; but business was heavy and I
was loafing about.

I drove the old man in Bill's car down the gravel road
for several miles, and finally turned up a disused drive to
a small unpainted house. I got out to help take in the
several boxes, and the man's wife came to the door. She
was small and dainty, with gray hair in wisps about her
head. The man said, "This here Mr. Bill's brother-in-law.
He brought me with the groceries."

"My," the old woman said, "but ain't he nice. And he
look just like Mr. Bill."

"No," the old man said, "he Mr. Bill's brother-in-law. He married to Mr. Bill's sister."

"My," the old woman said, "but ain't he handsome."

I spoke to her and carried in a box of groceries. "Ain't he nice, though?" she said as I passed her in the doorway. I put the groceries on a table in the dark kitchen and went out for some more. "And so good-looking," she said, as if I were out of earshot and these remarks were simply to herself. Her voice was small and smooth and placating. I was uncomfortable.

"He's so handsome," she said as I went back and forth past her. "So *nice*. My, just look how he do help! And so good-looking."

In recent years my connection with colleges has given me a sort of key to the educated Negro's world, and for the last few months of my recent three-year stint in Mississippi, I had from time to time the only relatively free conversation with Negro people that I have ever had in the South. At meetings, dinners, small suppers, educated and interested white people and Negroes talked about whatever they chose — this was not in the specific interest of biracial discussion at all — and I discovered that after an hour or so of such talk sometimes they seemed to forget I was white and I would no longer notice that they were black.

One additional year away, and when I returned my first encounters with Negroes were with those I hired to help me move my furniture from Mississippi to Louisiana. They talked to each other as they worked, but I was unable to understand what they were saying. Even when they talked to me, sometimes I had to ask and ask, and occasionally I never did decipher what it was they were telling me or asking me. I finally asked one of them to take over and direct the loading of the van. He did a perfectly capable, though unintelligible, job.

At the request of our local television station in Louisiana, I did a special program on Robert Frost shortly after his death. On campus the next day a number of people mentioned it to me, as is usual at so small a college. However dull or however removed from poetry the person was who mentioned the program, I was not surprised until two of the Negro janitors said something to me about it.

My surprise then shocked me. The two men had given some evidence of being the moral and intellectual superiors of many of our students and of some of our faculty and administration, yet it surprised me to have them say they liked my program on Frost. One of them said he learned a great deal from it.

Suddenly in my mind there was an entire black audience beyond the camera, an audience I had never thought of, not even subconsciously. Their world is so clearly, so subtly, separate from ours that a mutual interest in Robert Frost had never occurred to me. The separation lurks there, even in the minds of us who most believe that the barriers should be down.

Another Negro worker on the campus said a thing humorously that sticks in my mind with a broader application than he was allowing it. "I reckon it's a good thing I has so much bad luck," he said. "Cause if I didn't have bad luck, I wouldn't have no luck at all."

V

In Our Place

I don't know how far back into the varied past of Sicily a genealogist would have to trace before he discovered the most recent of my ancestors who was either a slaveowner or a slave. But the search would be brief on the American side of the family: my great-grandfather owned slaves. His son, my grandfather, I remember quite clearly, although he died when I was only seven.

In my grandfather's house, a few years after he died, I saw a woman who herself had been a slave and had been old enough when Emancipation came to remember slavery. She stood in the wide hallway straight and proud and in good spirits, talking with my grandmother while the rest of us watched, and the only thing that sticks in my mind besides a sharp image of her is that either she still had all her teeth or it was said that every tooth she had in her head was her own.

My grandparents' house was in the country in Leake County, Mississippi. That is, it was "in the country" to us, who lived near Jackson, the capital and largest city of the state, where some 50,000 people made their homes in one crowded area. However, to the people who lived yet farther out, in Leake County, as my great-uncle and many other kinsmen did, my grandparents lived in town. Town was Standing Pine, where two roads came together and a few stores were located: an average over the years, perhaps, of three general stores. While my grandfather lived, his small white office building was in use; later it was boarded up and now it is gone. A frame schoolhouse and a frame Baptist Church, each back among oak trees, stood some distance from the stores and each other. I can remember the loud beat of a gristmill beside the store nearest "home" during one period, and for a while, at least, someone had a pool table in one of the buildings; in minor ways things changed in Standing Pine as the depression played out and war was fought.

The town is in Choctaw Indian territory, and an Indian school is nearby. I used to be told that the Indian name for the town was Trickum. The stores were important until well within my own memory, and do some business yet, but although the roads are still not very good from Standing Pine to the highway, the larger stores of Carthage are only a few minutes away and Jackson, down the Natchez Trace Parkway, can be reached in an hour.

My own great fondness for Standing Pine may be beside the point, but some comprehension of such a community of farmers, storekeepers, schoolteachers and combinations of these (my grandfather was a farmer-preacher-doctor) living at some distance from each other along red dust roads difficult to negotiate by automobile after a rain, and across red clay fields of cotton, or pine and sweetgum thickets, or bitterweed-infested pastures — some comprehension of a relatively primitive life and a sense of some of its problems and its pleasures is necessary to any sort of understanding of Mississippi. It is in such areas generally that the background of thought has formed as the state has precipitated, more slowly than most of the nation, into small towns, and as it now is developing cities. My own background was small town and city, both from just outside; but my roots are in Standing Pine too.

We did not have to make a living there, and so when we were concerned about the weather it had little to do with whether the cotton would have enough rain to develop or a long enough dry season to ripen. We might want the thick red dust laid, but we never wanted so much rain that we could not drive up Scott Hill without sliding back into a great red gully of a ditch.

And we thought of the pasture land not in terms of cattle and the slim economics of living there, but of play: there were the pine groves where we could slide on barrel staves down the slopes covered with slick pine straw. There were the sweetgum trees with large grapevines hanging down to be climbed or swung on, and the special vine which rose briefly from the root, grew parallel with the ground for a couple of feet, and then went up to hang in the tree limbs, making a fine springy "horse" for us to fight over.

And there were the characters. Most of them we kids didn't really know, but their names were familiar: some of them identified what we would amount to if we didn't quit being so lazy. One woman was a great lover of Garrett's snuff, and she would chew a matchstem or a sweetgum twig to sop out the last bits in the bottom of the can.

She told my grandmother one day, "I just wisht I'd married old man Garrett hisself."

There was Standing Pine Creek, where my uncle took us swimming. There were the Barnett reunions on the packed dank clay underneath the oak trees, with tables made of boards on sawhorses, and with so many cakes we couldn't taste one of every kind without getting sick, but we tried.

We used to buy candy for a penny in a dark little store in town; once I got a new kind with thin air holes in it, and I didn't like it. I remember that I walked slowly through the pasture wondering if there were something seriously wrong about me, not liking candy. It was in the same pasture that my brothers and I played cars with my uncle's tobacco cans in the dusty mule wallow, and my younger brother started over the hill to the house just as a mule loped toward him, heading for the wallow. My brother was very small, but he outran the mule down the hill and across the wallow while my older brother and I rolled under the barbed wire fence in some terror and watched the mule give up what we had thought was a chase to roll over in the dust and flatten our Prince Albert cans.

White people as well as Negroes were tenant farmers in the area. I remember a white boy, son of a tenant farmer on the place one year. His language was what intrigued me. My father was a preacher, and nobody used questionable words around us, except for a few school-mates — and they were surreptitious, often hesitant, and inherently guilty. I had never heard anyone, if asked what he had said, repeat the curse words he had used, and being something of a moralist I made a point of asking this boy just to force him to correct himself.

"Look at that goddam cow," he would say.

"What did you say?" I would ask.

"Look at that goddam cow," he would repeat. He was always accurate in his repetitions. Apparently he was completely unaware of my attempted reproof.

I remember a Negro man who was a sharecropper there, too, although my memory is principally of an overheard conversation between him and his boss. He had knocked on the back steps and his employer had come to the door and said, "What do you want?"

"Yessuh. How you this evening? Wellsuh, I reckon I need a little money, if you got it to spare."

"How much?" The tone was gruff, but his tone was generally gruff to anybody.

"Wellsuh, I need ten dollars, right now. I needs to get some medicine . . ."

"Saturday night's coming up, and you want to get drunk. That's what it is."

"Nawsuh. That ain't it this time. It's this medicine. And then we out of cornmeal and there ain't no meat left . . ."

"Who you going out to get drunk with? That no-good John? He's going to get you in real trouble. You better just forget the ten dollars and stay home."

"Nawsuh, I ain't going out with no John. It's the medicine."

It went on, the badgering and the wheedling, until the ten dollars changed hands.

A kind of paternalism, often rough and often not, was the rule, of course, for years. In many ways it was an inevitable transition from the system of slavery, I suppose, since the slaves were simply released and left in the care of their former masters. And of course the Negro who was treated as if he were incapable of responsibility often took advantage of the situation not to have to feel or be responsible. The white man looked on him as a nigger; he would be one. Especially since there wasn't much else he could do anyway.

The word "nigger" was in the vocabulary in many ways. Some of us were discouraged from using it, or forbidden to use it, especially in the hearing of Negroes. But all of us heard "nigger" jokes, generally based on the inferiority of the race. One such dirty joke circulating in lowered tones when I was a boy had to do with a Yankee boy who came down for a visit, and his friends took him to a Negro prostitute. The Southern boys went first, and when the Yankee went in he was careful not to say anything and so betray his alien status. Finally, however, the Negro woman said, "You's from the Nawth, ain't you?" The boy said, "How did you find out? I came in here and didn't talk and did just what they did." "Yassuh," she said, "but they didn't kiss me." The underlying assumptions of the story were the underlying assumptions of most of its audience.

A more "innocent" use of the term "nigger" was in the counting rhyme:

> Eenie, Meenie, Meinie, Mo.
> Catch a nigger by his toe.
> If he hollers make him pay
> Fifty dollars every day.

And the slingshot was most commonly called a nigger-shooter, although I do not recall ever seeing one used to shoot Negroes. That was simply a term in the language, just as the Brazil nuts we would get in our stockings at Christmas were called niggertoes.

When my grandfather was dying, the grandchildren were sent to the home of a neighboring cousin where we jumped in freshly picked cotton in a little cotton house and played baseball on the hard clay yard. One child there was just to the age of speaking, and when at dinner he kept referring to the chocolate cake as "nittah cake" (his nearest approach to "nigger cake") we giggled behind our hands, because we thought that the little boy was funny, but also that it wasn't really nice to make that kind of reference. From an older person it would not have been funny.

Most nice white people felt no animosity toward the Negro people and actually considered it their duty to attend to those around them who had had particular misfortunes. But certain lines were drawn and were expected to be kept, especially by the "nice" white people. A white woman of superior intelligence and ability and of an outstanding family told me a few years ago of her experience during the depression after not only the depression itself, but a tornado and the physical disability of her husband had put the family into a critical financial situation and made it necessary for her to do something so that they would not starve. The only thing there was to do the federal government provided, and that was to make clothes for children on relief.

A group of women were hired at something like $8 a week, if my memory of her memory serves, to do the sewing, and there was one position available. The woman was told, however, that only Negro women were doing the work, and so of course she could not. She replied that she did not care in the slightest, that she wanted the job, that it was offered, and that she was going to have it. She got it. But there was some dissatisfaction. Further, it developed that the white woman who was in charge and had not wanted her to have the job was making some personal profit on the goods used. None of the Negro women would have dared report her, but it was apparent that this white woman with a will of her own and with high standing in the entire area by virtue of family might easily make trouble; besides, it was not really a nice situation, her working there with all those Negro women as if she were one of them, or trash, or something. And so my friend was found a better and more congenial job with an agency which, it turned out, dealt with Negroes, but not "with" them.

Actually, with the patronage of a strong white family and with some reserve or audacity, a Negro could achieve a certain kind of standing in a community. No other position could approximate it, because once the Negro had established his peculiar brand of independence, there was no avenue of approach to him. One had simply to keep his distance and to suffer whatever hauteur the Negro had the nature and the skill to sustain.

One such Negro was the butcher in a grocery store in the town where I grew up. The store itself was an ancient-looking thing, with peeling posters down its exposed brick side and with a warped tin awning over the sidewalk in front. Worn dark benches hung beneath the windows on each side of the door, and Negro men sat on them and chewed tobacco, presumably the brands advertised in the old posters and on the store windows; they watched the town, and talked intermittently. The store was even more dark and drab inside. It always frightened me just a little, because we did not trade there and I only went in once in a while with a friend. It was so dark that you could never really see into it through the windows or the screen door, and your eyes would have to adjust for a moment inside to make out the glass counter for candy and the bread racks.

Off to one side was a heavy glass meat counter, and behind that the Negro butcher stood with a white apron on. He did not smile and he did not move about placatingly and he did not nod just a bit too profusely. He stood there solidly and waited. He served you efficiently. I was told he was the best butcher around, but I was always just a trifle suspicious that this was said and believed so that the customer could justify his having been treated as an equal, or perhaps as an inferior. Many of the townspeople, I gathered, too, were as bound to this store by virtue of what they owed as many of the share-croppers in the delta were to the plantation commissary, and if they wanted meat, they pretty well had to pretend that the butcher was the best and that his distant, self-sufficient manner did not bother them in the slightest.

And the butcher did have a patron, in a fashion. The family who owned and operated the store was considered one of the "money" families in town, and it seemed to be assumed that to insult their butcher would mean to deal with them. I never did like him, myself. He made me uncomfortable. The whole place made me uncomfortable.

Among the nice ladies of those days, as I have indicated, little was ever said about the Negroes. Once in a while you might hear something to the effect that they simply were not as competent as they should be ("You can't trust them to do anything right, of course"), but it was normally said in a tone which betrayed little irritation and little disillusion, as if one were remarking on the inefficiency of a child who would never develop into adulthood.

It was quite a shock to me one day, then, about the end

of the depression, to hear the mother of one of my friends expend some real invective on Negro women. For years, it seems, she had been hiring help at $3 a week, entirely at her own discretion.

That was the set wage, and if she needed help she sent word to a Negro woman to come. If that one should be employed already by another white family, she would either send over a sister or a friend, or she would recommend someone who would then be told to come.

In recent months, however, things had changed. There were job openings, some apparently in industry and some as cleaning women in businesses and some for "better" homes, so that the wage situation had altered and availability had diminished. My friend's mother had been unable to get any help at all for $3 a week, and she had refused to pay more.

She complained bitterly. She said that it was those other jobs luring them away — perhaps she didn't say "from where they belong," but that was what she meant. She said that it just showed what no-good things they were. She said that they wanted $5 a week, and they had no right to ask it. They had no right to take jobs in the city for higher wages. They had no right not to come work for her at the wage of $3 a week when she needed them.

The argument seemed to me, a young adolescent, so spurious and unfeeling on the face of it that I was appalled. The woman was the wife of a man engaged in higher education and religion, a man of position and responsibility, of intellectual and moral leadership. I could hardly believe she could say such things. But apparently he agreed with her, and many educated, religious people really believed that she was right, although most of them would never say it in such a way. Rather, the observation became common that "They just don't seem to know their place any more." And references to the "good old Negroes, not like these young smarty ones today," haunted genteel nostalgia.

I suppose there were lynchings then in Mississippi, but I was hardly aware of such things. If I ever saw a Negro really abused verbally or physically until I was in college, I don't recall it. Even then I did not see it. I was inside the dormitory when an acquaintance of mine came in red and distraught and told about it. He was an upperclassman from somewhere in Mississippi, with little of what is generally thought of as the redneck about him. He was personable, his manner smooth — perhaps if anything a bit too smooth. He was steeped in the sort of Mississippi culture which makes it a virtue to maintain a sane, calm manner around all the less securely rooted elements of this world's society. And so his fury in itself was worth attention.

He told what had happened. He had been walking up the steps of the dormitory, whistling. A little Negro boy, possibly waiting for his father or mother who was working there, sat outside, and as the college boy went by, the Negro boy began whistling, too.

The college boy grabbed up a broom from somewhere and beat the little boy with it. Maybe that, he told us, would teach the little black son of a bitch to mock *him*.

VI

Even a Mule

A FEW YEARS ago a Michigan professor kindly offered to read a piece of my fiction set in a small Mississippi town. The things that struck him most immediately, he told me later, were three: the heat, the fact that people drank coffee all day long, and the way that everybody seemed to know immediately what happened anywhere in town.

The thing that struck me, in turn, was that he thought those things worth remarking on. I should not have been taken completely unawares, however; I had sat in his seminar room with the windows open and shivered in the 70-degree summer air while he complained about how muggy it was. Heat is a part of the South, and I grew up in it. Only in more recent years have I noticed it there particularly, and that perhaps because all the sizeable places of business, most of the classrooms, and many homes are now air conditioned, so that 95 degrees at 90 percent humidity on stepping outdoors is a severe physical blow.

Perhaps the constant coffee drinking is not peculiar to the South, although it has been common most places I have lived. Certainly the swift communication of events and rumors is typical of small towns everywhere.

The professor had never lived in a small town; I had never really lived anywhere else. And so he could sharpen my view of my own environment.

Clinton, the town I grew up near, where I went to school and church and where all my friends lived, is a rather old town for Mississippi. It was a mineral water resort in the early nineteenth century, and although almost all trace of that era is now gone, when I was a boy a few pre–Civil War remains were visible in addition to the old chapel at the college, which was still in use and has now been renovated. On our way to play in the sand gullies south of town, we used to pass a brick house with a few walls still upright, in one of which there were holes caused, according to legend, by pistol balls in a duel. In the yard a brick cistern was crumbling into itself. Locust trees shaded and sweetened the air.

Through some of the low hills nearby were cuts in the bottom of which we could clearly see the softened scorings of wagon wheels where the old Natchez Trace ran. Now the brown earth was weathered smooth and was blotched with scrubby grass, moss, and leaf mold.

North of town, there was another set of gullies, a semicircle washed out of a hillside to form a sand-clay cliff perhaps forty feet high, colored to our eyes like Grand Canyon. The spacious sandy bottom was surrounded on three sides by the cliffs, and when the ground was wet we used to have battles with wads of red and yellow clay from the walls; we would skulk behind little hillocks and small pines to besiege a balcony-like fort halfway up the cliffside.

Not far away, enclosed by an iron fence, was the grave of Cowles Meade, the man who is supposed to have captured Aaron Burr. It lay well off any road, hidden in pines. Farther out were the foundations and concrete steps of buildings which used to be a Negro school, established by some Northern sisters (as I remember the story) and named Dickey Institute after them. Their gravestones were close by; irises still grew around the outlines of the buildings and in rows out toward the graves. In spring, college students used to walk out to Dickey 'Stute and sit beneath the broad oaks. Honeysuckle covered many of the bushes, and the only sounds would be thrushes and mockingbirds and blue jays, and lizards darting through the decaying winter leaves.

Few houses were out that far except for those on small farms. Most of the Negro houses were back from the gravel roads far enough not to be seen or scarcely to be noticed, blending their gray, weathered planks into the scrub locusts and chinaberry trees and the worn, packed dirt. Pasture land and a dairy, cotton farms, and several houses with gardens of corn and beans and tomatoes lay close in to the railroad, beyond which was the town. The gravel roads turned into streets at the railroad, streets paved for the most part with bricks. From the depot the streets went uphill to the main part of town past an old store, a blacksmith shop, a mill which made cornmeal and feeds, some small homes and a couple of large old colonial houses set back behind pecan trees or ancient, peeling cedars. At the corner at the top of the hill was "town," with grocery stores a few doors in each direction, the bank, the post office, a drugstore, a couple of doctors' offices.

The bank was a local one at that time; now it is the

modern branch of a Jackson bank. I have heard an account of a depression-days meeting of the directors of the bank for the discussion of certain loans. The man who ran the bank had a reputation for being tight-fisted, but according to this account it was he who saw most of the Negro families through the depression, lending them money against their crops. He had made one such loan, and a highly respected director, a man slow of speech and very deliberate, began to comment on the loan. "Well," he said heavily, and paused. "I don't think . . ." He paused heavily again.

The other man broke in: "Of course not! You never thought in your life. That's what's the matter with you, you old fool!"

One little grocery store, just under the hill, was the favorite of us boys, because whenever we bought candy there, the grocer would scoop it up in a little barrel measure, and then heap it as high as it would go. Surely the store had some other business, but all I ever saw was the penny candy sales; and we were not so affluent then as to have a penny every day.

There was a shoe shop, a cleaning shop, and an old store building of brick with huge boarded windows and doors, and with the story that the town drunk, or one of the town drunks, lived somewhere up inside it.

The doctors' offices had separate waiting rooms for white and Negro patients.

At that time the only churches in town were the large Baptist church and the smaller Methodist church, both well attended. A Baptist college was the principal feature of the town and contributed greatly to the size of the Baptist church. During revival time every year all the students at the local consolidated school were allowed to attend morning services if they wished.

The Negro janitor often sat in on worship services. One side of the balcony had classrooms off a corridor which was separated from the auditorium, as the main balcony was, by a low wooden banister and, higher, a brass rail. The janitor would usually move a folding chair out of a classroom and sit back of the railing. Occasionally there would be, perhaps for a funeral, four or five Negroes in the back of the balcony.

Across the highway was the college with its brick buildings and elm trees. A gray World War I cannon stood at the entrance. Near the chapel there were a couple of old cedars; on the best days their dark green and the rich red patina of slave-made bricks were backed by a deep blue sky.

Across town, near the railroad track, there was a girls' two-year college, originally Central Female Institute, but long named Hillman College after its "Northerner" president who is supposed to have persuaded Grant to spare both colleges. Hillman was green lawn and shade trees, a couple of large white frame buildings, and a few houses. Every Sunday morning, led by a chaperon, the girls walked double file to church in light summer dresses (at least it is perpetual early summer in my memory of that ritual), and the college boys stood around the high side steps of the church and waited.

The Negro church, the only one I knew of, was at the edge of town, toward our house and Jackson. Across the street, the Negro cemetery was often weed-grown and always scant in visible tombstones. Adjoining it, back toward town, the white cemetery lay neatly mowed, a sedate forest of marble among the heavy green leaves and sweet white flowers of Cape jessamine.

At the principal corner between the college and the cemeteries was a Chevrolet agency which gained some aura of romance for us boys. It was during and just after the days when we used to "play like" the first streamlined cars of the thirties were the getaway vehicles of John Dillinger or Pretty Boy Floyd and as they passed riddle them with our make-believe submachine guns. The garage was the most prosperous-looking place on the highway, and since it was in a sleepy small town passing burglars would stop by to pick up some apparently easy cash. Unfortunately for them, it had a burglar alarm, and the brothers who owned it would be able from their houses to cover opposite corners with shotguns while help was summoned. I don't believe anybody ever successfully robbed the place.

Once as soon as I arrived at school my friends hurried me down to the garage because burglars had broken in the night before and one man, opening a large side window from the back work room in an attempt to escape, had been shot dead. They showed me the gravel he fell on and the shattered window, and then they took me in the back door. Some of the burglars had hidden in or under cars in the work area and had waited to be flushed out. It was very dark inside after the bright sunshine outdoors, and soon I began to notice that my eyes were burning and watering. My friends had not told me that tear gas had been used to encourage the burglars' exit; although the place had been airing for several hours, the residue left me teary for the rest of the morning.

The only other violence or outlawry in Clinton I can recall had to do with, once, some young people's breaking into a large old house and taking some things, or breaking them. Most of the offenders apparently got off with an admonition, and their names were never released, except for a couple whose families were insufficiently prominent to rate protection. And, in a series of incidents, the fighting and raiding that went on at sports events and on campus because of the rivalry between Mississippi College and Millsaps, the Methodist college in Jackson.

Racial trouble was unheard of, except that I do recall a retired professor who told my sixth grade class about the Negro uprisings of Reconstruction times, but that seemed so remote and he so ancient that I cannot now remember any more than the fact of his telling us. And I heard once a disapproving comment concerning a town marshal who was said to shoot craps with the Negroes and run them in if he lost.

After World War II the town was well on its way to tripling in size; the business area increased and dispersed; the city limits moved out; many new subdivisions opened up; the college began to quadruple; affluence began to seep in. A trailer village for veterans sprang up and deteriorated on the bank of the college's Lake Wilson, and Lake Wilson itself disappeared beneath a highway bypassing town. The old grade school's square three stories were leveled for a ranging one-story elementary school; the new high school grew old and crowded, and became the junior high school when the recently new high school was built in the leveled Piney Woods. All the surrounding area used to be pastureland and second growth oaks but is now solid middle-class homes, many with a sleek boat in the second garage. A shopping center is going up on the old highway toward Jackson, far out beyond the Negro church and the cemeteries, which are now relatively downtown.

So, to some extent, has it gone in all nine of the small Southern towns I have lived in since World War II.

The only two incidents concerning race that I recall during the war occurred in San Diego, where I tried to suppress my wonder at seeing a Negro man and white woman walking along together, and in a tent on Mindoro in the Philippines, where I recall shouting vehemently at one of my crew members from New York because he kept talking about the Jiggaboos and how they were all no good. I was brought up separate, but as a fact, not as a creed.

After the war I returned to college in my old home town, and there was, as many people insist, some slight difference in the relationship between the races, at least in the abstract. We young college students, the ones interested in something in addition to football and courtship, talked about the racial situation a great deal, generally agreeing, at least in certain groups, that the degradation of the Negro was our fault, that something should be done about it, and that maybe we ought to be the ones to do it. Some half dozen friends of mine once wrote a letter to the editor of a Jackson paper criticizing the Dixiecrats, who were running strong at the time, and signed their names. The letter was printed, and the boys got some mail in return. I knew of a couple of abusive letters, one written as if from a Negro prostitute to the Nigger Lovers and drowning them in degenerate endearments.

One of the boys showed me the letter. He was virtually never serious, and so when he handed me the letter and I read it and then looked up to see a completely solemn face I was for the moment nonplussed. "They're just persecuting me because I'm a Jew," he said. I went into hysterics, partly because in spite of his name it had never occurred to me that he was a Jew, and mostly because obviously he was being assaulted because he had challenged White Supremacy. Fortunately, he was never able to resist laughter.

Our student newspaper, the *Collegian,* was at that time reasonably free, and I wrote a column in it with what might be called impunity. In a couple of columns I satirized the racists, and so far as I can recall there was no negative response — little response at all. But I also parodied some of the faculty and administration without being censured. The only one of the columns that elicited a counterattack was a rather biting parody of the overzealous in religion. A note was posted on the chapel bulletin board to the effect that, among other things, I needed salvation. Several ministerial students preached to the girl who was editor and to a girl I had dated recently; but nothing adverse was said directly to me. Journalism in the Southern schools has often been somewhat free, though not in some other years even on the paper for which I wrote. Ole Miss, through all its recent crises, has had a free student newspaper. The Southern college at which I taught last removed its editor for a remark about the cafeteria.

I understand there were some tense moments, however, over the college magazine about the time I was writing, as an undergraduate, for the *Collegian*. The editor ran a cartoon, as I recall, of a Negro being crucified. Perhaps it was because it hit on both sore spots at once, but an upheaval took place following that issue. Nevertheless, many of the students were in favor of just such journalism, and none of us thought to look over our shoulders before saying that we thought the Negro had the same rights we had, or an equal ability, or a comparable purpose in the world. Perhaps this sense of freedom was the result of our being students, and so being considered too young and unconnected with things to matter; and maybe we knew this too. Certainly ours was not the prevailing sentiment by any means, and I recall Hodding Carter's direct and intelligent speech at the Southern Literary Festival

of 1948 as being so obviously opposed to the general attitudes of the time that some of us were poised to rush up
at the conclusion and defend him against violence. We
had never heard an older person come out publicly and
say what Carter dared to say, although it was what we
had been saying less well. Instead of attacking him, however, the audience of selected student writers from various
schools in the South applauded so long and vehemently
that it seemed to embarrass him.

One summer I lived in the home of an elderly couple
at the edge of a small Mississippi delta town. The delta is
a broad area of rich, black land along the Mississippi
River; it is there that the large plantations still exist, and
the Negroes required to work the cotton, before automa-
tion began its inroads even there, were so numerous that
in some counties the white people are a small minority,
and the ruling white people an even smaller minority.
This town is at the rim of the delta, just before the hill
country rises suddenly out of the flat land into a quite
different sort of world.

The couple lived in a large white house with a veranda
around two sides of it and with large trees shading the
yard. The old man would sit in the swing at the corner
of the veranda, where it was nearly always cool. He liked
to talk, and I would sit there with him when I had time.
His children had grown up with varying degrees of success; he and his wife were alone, and although they were
obviously fond of each other and got along pleasantly,
they missed having the boys around, and so they treated
me as if I were their own.

I contracted only for a room, but my landlady was concerned about my health and insisted on making breakfast
for me every morning. She refused to take additional

money for it, and she refused to abandon the scheme:
I needed a good breakfast to start off the day. I got it.
She gave me juice, a bowl of hot oatmeal, eggs and bacon,
and what sometimes seemed to me half a loaf of bread
toasted. I went to work stuffed for the morning.

The old man had for years made his living by ped-
dling a line of vanilla and baking powder and hair tonic
and such to the Negroes, traveling the whole area year
after year, so that he was well acquainted with the Negro
people. Retired now, he would sit in his swing and occasionally sell a bottle of perfume or a box of talcum powder
to a Negro who would come up to the picket fence and
respectfully call out a request; his manner with customers
was always short, although he did keep some goods on
hand and did continue to accept money for them.

In many ways he was an interesting old man; he had
little education, but his observations were often clear and
intriguing. He had lost an eye and an arm to cancer, but
he did not complain. Instead, he talked with admiration
about the cancer clinic where the parts had been removed
and his life saved.

The day I moved in, I carried from my car a pair of
ebony busts my sister had sent me from Nigeria. The little
figures are perhaps three inches high, a man and a woman
carved in black wood. As I passed my host, who was sitting in the swing, he looked at them fixedly. "Where you
taking them niggers?" he said.

"Into my room," I answered, and walked on. Obviously,
he had not been pleased, but he said nothing else about
my "niggers."

I soon discovered that he did not dislike Negroes. He
hated them. He had spent most of his life dealing almost
exclusively with Negroes day in and day out, and all the

while he hated them. Negroes and religion were his two aversions, and so far as I could determine those two things absorbed all his hatred.

One of his favorite stories, which he told with considerable malice and pleasure, concerned a picnic of some years before sponsored by the Adult Union of the local Baptist Training Union, or BTU, as it was called. One man, enjoying the food, loudly complimented the cooks by saying, "You BUT ladies put on quite a spread."

It was in the same area that a Women's Missionary Union circle discussed, as per the literature that came to them from headquarters, the problem of race and the necessity of looking on all men as precious in the sight of God, and so on. At the end of the lesson, which had been gone through faithfully and without question, one of the women was asked to close the meeting in prayer. "Oh, Lord, help us to be good to the Negroes," she prayed, "even though they aren't as good as we are."

One year a friend and I taught a night school for veterans who were trying to get their high school diplomas and, more especially, the GI Bill money. Most of them were from the country around the small town (this was in the hills) and had grown up in the real South; but they had gotten away from it during the war. Some of our discussions necessarily ranged over the race problems of the state, and my friend and I both being liberal, the students often tried to be as understanding as possible for our sakes. Some few really were. But the comment that stands out in my mind is one by a boy who had been stationed for a while at the same base as Joe Louis, and had been, he said, convinced that Joe Louis was really a nice guy: he hadn't acted stuck up and biggity.

Some people were not blind to the fact of their inherent

prejudices, however. One of the best school men I have
ever known was superintendent of schools where I taught
for a couple of years. He ran an excellent white school,
and apparently was doing a good job of overseeing the
Negro schools, too. I learned a great deal about teaching
and about dealing with young people from him. His was
not a one-level mind. He told me once, because of a
problem that had become intensified in the attempted
solution, that the trouble with the principal was that he
could see only one response to any difficulty, when of
course there were a thousand possibilities to be weighed.

He weighed possibilities, and when it came to the question of improving the Negro schools, partly by contracting
for a new building at considerable cost to the white tax-
payers, since the Negroes had little money or property
to be taxed, he fought an unpopular battle for the new
school, and won. The argument he used in reply to opponents was that even a mule is of more use to us if it is
trained.

Such a remark was made, by this man, not in ignorance.
He knew precisely the effectiveness and the implications
of the argument. He told me that he used such an approach only because it was all that certain people could
understand. He believed in a better education for the
Negroes on other grounds. Nevertheless, having grown
up in the most remote area of a rural hill county, he continued with his usual honesty, no matter how he tried
he could not make himself believe that the Negro was
either equal or potentially equal to the white man.

Even during the period when the relationship between
the races was to whatever slight extent relaxed, then,
attitudes were basically the same as they had been, and
the Negro was neither thought of nor treated as equal in
nature or in rights to the white man.

When the Negro took the same sort of liberties that many white men could take with impunity, the Negro found immediately that he had gone too far. I have tried in vain to remember exactly what happened in a Mississippi town one night during the friendly era. The bus carrying the high school band had had a flat tire, and the driver pulled into a service station to have it fixed. I was along as a chaperon, and I got out with some of the boys to stand around in the cool air and wait.

A car pulled in with the front end battered. It was a black Buick, I believe, and there were several Negroes inside. The driver got out and said that they had run into a mule that had charged out of the darkness onto the highway, and he wanted to get in touch with the marshal and report the accident and perhaps make a complaint against the owner of the mule for letting it out.

The night marshal appeared, and the Negro man began his report. He was shaken from the accident, and as he went along he used vulgarity with increasing frequency and intensity. It seemed that he was getting a sympathetic hearing, and apparently that inspired him to get the whole thing out of his system with a big gush of anger and relief in the camaraderie of masculine talk.

Finally the marshal broke in very abruptly and said for him to shut up that kind of language. The Negro man looked around and said that he didn't see any ladies present, and the marshal either cursed him and ran him away or hit him and ran him away. I can't remember which; all I can remember is the shock, the fact that whatever it was could not happen. But it did.

VII

White Heaven

At a county teachers' meeting in Oxford, Mississippi, many of the older members seemed to feel impelled to make some sort of verbal protest against the troubles soon to result from the new Supreme Court decision against segregation in the schools. Their remarks were random and inconclusive, and to us restless younger teachers the air seemed heavy and plaintive.

There had been many wise mutterings full of vague but dire portents when finally someone complained, "Next they'll be wanting to come to our churches."

The teacher sitting next to me whispered, "Afraid they'll get into white heaven."

Since that time numerous barriers have been raised in the South between the Negro and white heaven. The one incident which stands in my mind as the most ironic took place in Kentucky. I do not mean to imply that the irony arises from its not having happened in Mississippi — the circumstances which brought it about could not themselves have existed in Mississippi: an "integrated" college was one necessary ingredient.

It was about the time that Louisville was being praised, no doubt justly, for its orderly tradition to integrated schools, and people who thought Louisville was really in the South were optimistic for Mississippi and Alabama too.

The Kentucky town I lived in was also beginning its orderly integration of the public schools. But benighted as they are, the schools are often closer to intelligence than the churches are to love. My father used to make a clear distinction in his sermons between "religion" and "Christianity," and I have some such distinction in mind when I say that the South in general, and particulary within its churches, is devoutly religious but, like everywhere else, largely un-Christian.

And so it was that a fascinating situation developed in a Baptist church as a result of its proximity to a Baptist college, and as a result of the missionary program which is fundamental to Baptist doctrine and practice.

The college was integrated. That is, a few Negroes were enrolled, though their number seemed to be deliberately limited and locale was apparently a factor in that only local Negroes were attending; as nearly as possible dormitory problems should be avoided.

The college was very missionary-minded, however, and so when some missionaries to Nigeria sent two Nigerian men to be trained in a Southern Baptist institution of higher learning and to study firsthand Southern Baptist church methods, the college accepted them. I believe they were even housed in one of the dormitories.

The problem arose when the two men wanted to attend church. The local church had "sent out" the particular missionaries who had in turn sent the Nigerians back, and the church was supporting those missionaries and the entire effort to win the world to the Southern Baptist way. But the people who were won to the Southern Baptist way could not, it was decided by some church officials, become members of that Southern Baptist church.

The Nigerians were allowed to attend the church, provided that they sat in a prescribed place and provided that they wore some distinguishing portion of their tribal regalia so that it would be readily apparent that they were not local Negroes. Such a distinction would make them more or less palatable to the members of the church and would keep alive the understanding on the part of the local Negroes that they, being local and so not transitory, were not welcome.

Soon, however, the Nigerians realized that they could hardly study Southern Baptist methods at firsthand by sitting in prescribed seats in tribal regalia. They must enter actively into the church. It was suggested to them that there were in the town Negro Baptist churches in which they could work closely with the entire congregation and learn church methods with no difficulty. But they discovered that these were not Southern Baptist churches at all and that the entire setup of the Negro churches differed considerably from the churches they had been sent to study.

Some of the college professors, at some peril to their jobs from the administration which had admitted the Nigerians but did not want a fight with the church, took up the cause of the Nigerians, and through many long, emotional meetings of the board of deacons and the church (the Southern Baptist church is even more demo-cratic in structure and ideal than the United States, but as in any institution the people don't often get a chance at a real decision unless they insist and insist and insist) these professors and some other members succeeded at length in allowing the Nigerians to join the church.

Perhaps the greatest irony of all is that apparently the Nigerians still wanted to.

The question with some Southerners has not been whether or not the Negro will get into white heaven — if my friend's remark about white heaven is taken literally its bite will be lost — but what he will be like there. A few years ago I was more or less party to a conversation between two brothers of about sixty. We sat in the rela-tively cool shade of a broad front porch in cane-bottom rocking chairs and a slat swing, and the conversation con-sisted of one man's comment on any subject and the immediate response: "No. That ain't so."

Eventually the talk got around to race, and one brother remarked with a kind of genuine charity an outsider would likely mistake, "Well, there's one thing. When we get up to heaven we'll all be the same."

"No," the other said. "That ain't so."

"Yes, it is, too. There wont be any black or white in heaven. We'll all be the same."

"No. No, sir. That ain't so. They'll still be black in heaven."

"How do you know that?" the first said. "There's no place in the Bible that says so."

"Yes there is, too."

"No there ain't. You just show me."

The other man sat thinking hard for a long moment, and then his face lit up. "Yes, there is, too. The Bible says we'll know each other in heaven, and if one of 'em was black down here and wasn't black up there, I wouldn't know him!"

Negroes are to be distinguished not only by color in heaven and preferably by tribal regalia in the church, but in the language everywhere. There is some sort of hierarchy of reference among the terms Negro, nigger, colored person, and darky. I have never been sure of the precise distinctions, since usages vary according to the basic attitudes of the white people speaking as well as according to their judgment of the particular Negro referred to. And of course usage varies according to the locale and social position of the speaker as well. Nevertheless, darky seems to carry connotations of Uncle Tomism, and on the part of the white speaker an approving paternalism. Nigger shows neither approval nor respect of any kind, unless it is used with the kind of grudging admiration one might express by such an exclamation as, "That son of a bitch sure can run." The word Negro (or as those who attempt dialect often spell it, Nigra) is used as a designation which, according to the speaker, either carries respect, indicates neutrality, or means to remove the speaker from any hint of prejudice. Colored man or colored woman seems to be as mild an appellation as the Southerner (of course, as the term is used all Southerners are white) has come up with, which still, as is necessary to him, distinguishes race.

Not long after the discussion of color in heaven, I was informed that we have been wrong in the use of one of these terms all along. "Black's not a color and white's not a color," I was told. "Black is the absence of color and white is all colors combined. So they're not colored people. Now, the Indians and the Chinese can be called colored people, but not the Negroes."

Whatever we called the Negroes in Mississippi and the South, when the Supreme Court desegregation decision came almost all Southerners reacted against it. Even the old separate-but-equal show, calculated to serve as a defensive compromise, met with some real opposition. The Alabama college at which I taught in 1955 was apparently considered as a possible sacrifice. It would be made a Negro college, according to rumor, and be used to demonstrate the good will of Alabama so that real desegregation would not be insisted upon, regardless of the Supreme Court. But one prominent townswoman was reported as saying rather openly that when they made the college a Negro college, she would be the first to put a match to it.

It may have seemed to some of us futile and insane, as well as undemocratic and illegal, to resist integration, but at whatever cost Mississippi did resist with complete success for another eight years, and the degree of integration achieved then was, of course, numerically almost invisible and socially even less perceptible.

On the other hand, some sort of unofficial integration has gone on, for years, often deliberately unnoticed, at Tougaloo College near Jackson. The faculty has been integrated, and at least some integrated meetings have taken place there. One such meeting caused a real uproar, however, a few years after desegregation was decided against in this country.

A class from Millsaps College, the white Methodist college in Jackson, met with a class of Negro students from Tougaloo for some kind of joint study. It was reported that they were segregated within the room, but nevertheless some influential Millsaps supporters raised the devil about it. Millsaps withstood the onslaught; the bishop, the president, the dean, and the involved professor held firm on the grounds of academic freedom, although the

professor was subjected for some time to personal harassment and threats and the college to abuse and loss of
prospective funds.

The newspapers were full of the story, and all other
colleges were rapidly and nervously trying to make sure
they would not become, through some irresponsible professor, the target of so violent an attack from their own
alumni and supporters.

From the rival college, where there was some snickering
at the discomfiture of our neighbor, I watched Millsaps
with admiration and gratitude. And so it was that one
morning when our public relations man brought his cup
of coffee to the next table in the cafeteria, I hailed him
with the question: "Why is it that Millsaps is getting all
the good publicity?" He was almost into his seat, but he
stood up abruptly and looked around in alarm. Then he
laughed nervously at what he thought was my little joke.

Millsaps did weather the storm, and within two years
the offending professor was again being asked to speak at
service clubs. That battle was won, but the war, of course,
was so far from over that one wonders if it will not be lost
through unpublicized attrition.

While the Millsaps uproar was still loud, a columnist for
the *Clarion-Ledger,* Jackson's and the state's largest newspaper, wrote about it. He apologized for meddling in
Methodist affairs, since he was not a Methodist, but he
had been asked by a Methodist legislator to comment
upon the situation. He took up the argument that college
students should hear two sides of things, and dismissed
it. Might as well, he said, bring in prostitutes or inmates
of the state penitentiary to give the other side. We didn't
send our children to college to hear both sides; we sent
them to learn what is right.

He went on to say that the mingling of the races is

obviously wrong. If God had meant for white people and Negroes to intermingle, He would have made them the same color. The redbirds and bluebirds do not cross-breed.

It is possible that even the breeders of cattle in the state were able to look at redbirds and bluebirds, nod sagely, and turn the Black Angus bull in with the lighter cows. Perhaps even the bird watchers were not aware that redbirds and bluebirds fail to cross-breed less because of their high degree of racial pride and moral integrity than because they can't. And even the ministers may have envisoned a God whose reasoning would prompt Him to prevent hybridization by creating a discrepancy in skin color rather than in reproductive organs. In any case, the same columnist still writes the same kind of material for his daily audience of Mississippians.

Not all newspapermen in the state were so illogical, however, at least in private. One rather prominent editor complained in my hearing that on the one hand we accuse the Negroes of being sexually immoral and we malign them for disdaining marriage and respectability, yet when they do get married we refuse to put Mr. and Mrs. before their names in the newspapers.

Still another editor complained to me one day at some length about the supposed segregationists who were so hot and bothered about whether or not they had to sit by a Negro on a bus or in school or in a restaurant, and yet at the same time practiced the much more intimate form of integration involved in turning over to the Negroes the most vital parts of the household: the kitchen and the bathroom. They would yell about being afraid of disease from sitting by Negroes, and then have a Negro girl in the house all day preparing the food and using the same bathroom.

I was just before congratulating him on puncturing an-

other segregationist myth when he went on vehemently
to say that he, now, was a *real* segregationist; he'd be
damned if he would have any Negro girl putting her
hands in *his* food or her black fanny on his toilet seat.

About this same time a young man of my acquaintance
appeared in Jackson one night in some agitation. He had
been visiting over the weekend in his home town in another part of the state, and there had been a killing.
According to the account he had, a particular white man
from nearby had been driving down a road in his pickup
truck and had been delayed by a stalled car belonging to
a Negro man. The white man got out of the pickup truck,
shot the Negro, got back in, and drove off.

The white man had killed, according to common knowledge, several Negroes. Never had he been arrested. This
recent corpse would not be listed as a fatality. No records, no crime.

The young man who told me the story was horrified.
This was his home town, and he knew of nothing to do
about it. What should be done? He didn't know. I didn't
know.

Incidents began to make it clear to me that, even
though the postwar years had not been really much better
than the prewar years, the post–1954 years were in many
ways worse. One day I stopped not far from my driveway
and offered a ride to an ancient Negro man. He was tall
and gave the appearance of being heavy, though he was
not much more than skin and bones. His clothes were
drab and dirty, as if they had been on him day and night
for weeks. His shoes were dark and worn and heavy. He
smelled of aged grime. It was very slowly that he walked,
and he got into the car with difficulty.

I had seen him before, and it seemed to me a quite traditional act of compassion or kindness or, more likely, old-fashioned paternalism to drive him to the store. I was surprised, then, when a few days later a neighbor took care to tell me that she had seen me pick up the old man, and that she wanted to thank me for it. She spoke of it as if it were a brave deed. Before 1954, who would have thought not to do it?

I note rather by the way that some few weeks later I was told of an old Negro man's having been found dead in a field where a day or two earlier he had been walking toward our new subdivision and, apparently, through it to town.

At the college, near which I had grown up and from which I had graduated and at which I was now teaching, chapel was compulsory. And so when I had the relative freedom of facultyhood I avoided chapel exercises as much as possible, and thereby I missed hearing with my own ears an older colleague tell the joke about the NAACP's having established a sit-in at Cape Canaveral because there were no Negro astronauts, their objective being, he said, a coon to the moon by June.

"Darky" jokes had been acceptable all through my memory, but such supposed humor as this, although even now not acceptable to the teachers who reported it to me, would not have been attempted at an earlier time.

During my last year or so in Mississippi, I became acquainted with some of the Tougaloo faculty and attended various functions there and spoke there once myself. It was no surprise to me to discover when I received a Danforth Teacher Study Grant in 1960 that a young Negro teacher from Tougaloo had also received one. The grant was much sought after, and I was the only successful nominee my college had ever come up with. And so

it was with some pride that I was presented at faculty
meeting one day as the only 1960 recipient of the grant
from Mississippi.

Perhaps Tougaloo was simply overlooked in the list —
but after 1954, especially, I could not help wondering.

The next year I spent distant from the South though
never removed from consideration of the problems of the
South, and then I returned as far as Louisiana. Getting
established in a new system and new courses took up
much of the first Louisiana year, along with several re-
writings of a musical satire. It was in indirect connection
with the production of the musical in Shreveport, Louisiana, the following summer that I observed at firsthand
some of the white attitude toward the Negro.

I traveled the 120 miles to Shreveport regularly by bus,
spent the week at work on the play as it went into production, and returned home on weekends. As I boarded
the bus one Monday in Alexandria, I saw that a young
Negro man was sitting on the right-hand side of the bus,
beside the window, only three or four seats from the front
instead of in the back of the bus as was customary and as
until recently had been according to law.

The fact of his presence there not only frightened me
somewhat, but also presented me with an awkward decision: where, then, should *I* choose to sit. It was to be
presumed that no one else on the bus was actively sympathetic either to him or to his cause, if any. That put some
responsibility upon me. The bus was relatively empty. I
could sit beside him, but there was no "natural" reason
for doing so, and it was possible that he did not want me
to in any case. It was further possible that my sitting
beside him would be the cause of a flare-up of violence.

I could walk on back and dissociate myself from him,

except that, of course, I couldn't. And so I sat across the aisle from him and thought that here at least I could keep an eye on things — a futile sort of gesture on the face of it. I discovered that although nothing was out of the ordinary except the Negro's presence "out of his place" and the possibility of incident, I was breathing rapidly and my heart beat with uncomfortable strength and volume. I wondered what he must feel and marveled at his apparently relaxed reading of a newspaper.

The bus driver went about his business as if nothing were unusual, and so did the other passengers until the bus reached Natchitoches. There a number of people boarded the bus; most of them went on to the middle of the bus, chose seats, and sat quietly. One rather young couple sat immediately in front of the Negro man, but without noticing his presence, it seemed, until they were seated. Then the woman, sitting at the window directly in front of the young Negro, turned sharply and looked at him. He continued to read the paper. The woman was a blonde with newly arranged hair in tight curls.

"Well!" she said very loudly. "What's this?" She punched her husband with gross gestures and pointed back at the Negro. The husband looked properly indignant. The woman yelled to a friend who had taken a seat somewhere behind me.

"Looks like we took the wrong bus!"

The friend answered something hardly intelligible.

"What is he?" The woman shouted again. Her voice was strident with righteousness. "A freedom rider or something?" She poked at her husband, a beefy-faced young man, and he turned in his seat with vague determination. I was in a constant state of turmoil inside, glowering at them and waiting to see what they would

do and then what I would do. The young Negro man re-
mained as nonchalant and aloof as if he had heard
nothing. The husband looked as if he might do whatever
it was his wife seemed to demand of him if only he knew
what it was and could get about it before he could realize
what a fool he was being.

The woman yelled some more to the friend behind me,
the husband stirred and reddened a time or two more, and
then the bus settled down to near normal. I was so dis-
gusted and so incensed at the indecency of the blond
woman that I could not keep from watching her with dis-
approval for some miles. Soon I realized that she and her
husband were consulting from time to time and glancing
back to where I sat in my protective position just opposite
the offending freedom-rider-or-something, and it occurred
to me at length that they had me pegged as an NAACP
official or Justice Department observer or other odious
creature put there to see to it they did not give the Negro
what he so richly deserved. Eventually they left off even
looking at me.

When we reached Shreveport, the people on the front
of the bus began to unload, and a few came on through
from the back. I got my bag and watched closely, but
nothing seemed likely to erupt until the Negro man moved
out into the aisle in his turn. Some distance behind him
was a very large redneck-looking man in work clothes,
and in my imagination I could see him suddenly enraged
at this nigger stepping out into the aisle in front of him
after riding ahead of him all this way, and so I blocked the
aisle behind the Negro with my suitcase, stopping the
white man, who showed no evidence at all of any of the
emotions I had imagined him, and I got off behind the
Negro. And that was it.

Toward the end of the summer I boarded the bus in Shreveport one morning after a long week and sleepless night with the play. I sat in approximately the same place that the young Negro man had occupied some weeks earlier, and I had already dozed off when someone asked me if the aisle seat beside me were available. I looked up to see a tall young Negro man. I said, "Sure. Sit down," and we talked briefly. He was living in the North and was on his way to Alexandria for a visit home. He said he would really be glad to get home again. I was doubtful that he would make it home with that feeling intact. He was sitting not only near the front of the bus, but with a white man.

I dozed off again, but when the driver called out our stop at Natchitoches, I became wide awake. A number of people got off the bus, and then I watched each person who came aboard, and waited. Nothing at all happened. When we parted in Alexandria he was apparently still happy to be home.

Still later, on the same bus route I sat beside a Negro man near the back of the bus. Ahead of me was a white man in a cheap suit; he had piled some boxes in the window seat beside him — I suspected as much to keep Negroes out as because the boxes were too big for the baggage rack. I was sure he would disapprove heartily of my sitting beside the Negro.

However, when he saw that I too had baggage troubles, he insisted that I put my bulky tape recorder on top of his boxes, and he kept it balanced for the fifty miles or more until the bus cleared somewhat. The Negro man beside me got off, and the white man shifted the tape recorder into the seat beside his boxes and sat with me, chatting amiably the rest of the way to Alexandria.

There was, then, some hope, it seemed to me. But the problems even there — not in Mississippi, but in a similar area of Louisiana — were far, far from solved.

On Halloween night our particular area was a prime target for trick-or-treaters. There was only one entrance, and the road (a city street) circled the mile or so around a lake. A single row of houses surrounded the lake, facing it across the road. It was a safe place for children to go from door to door, and since some of the homes were large it was considered a section where the handouts would be liberal. Cars would pull up to the entrance, across the street from the Negro section which fronted the area, and parents would wait while the kids made their haul. Many of the cars came from some distance.

We had heard echoes through our children of a neighbor's complaint about Negro children among the goblins the year before, but we largely discounted the concern as mere talk. For the first part of the evening, while I waited for a friend who had volunteered to get me off at eight o'clock on a necessary trip, I helped hand out candy. The kids came in all sorts of regalia, from store-bought shiny cloth representations of television cartoon characters to grocery sacks with holes cut for eyes. They came in all sizes, from toddlers to teenagers. Little groups would come trudging or galloping down the road with their trick-or-treat bags already filling; through the big windows that made up the front of our house we would watch them approach the door timidly or exuberantly; most of them would say "Thank you" when we gave them candy. Just before my friend arrived to pick me up, a few very small Negro children came across the lawn to the door. They must have ranged slightly under and over six years old, and none of them was in costume. They had made no attempt to disguise themselves, and they were open-faced, pleasant and polite. We gave them candy, they thanked us, and we watched them go on back across the lawn to the road. We assumed they were from just across the main road from the lake complex, and hence much nearer home than most of our visitors and much less prone to mischief than the ebullient fifteen-year-old white boys who had preceded them.

My friend arrived, I told my family goodbye, and we started to the car. Before we got out the door, we noticed a group of small children trotting along the roadside toward the entrance just ahead of a slow-moving car; they were dimly visible by the car's headlights. We wondered, made half speculations, and my friend and I hurried on to his car. When we pulled out to the entranceway we saw that a police car was sitting there; it had just herded the little Negro children out of our area and across the road.

In some of my classes at the college I asked each student to find some poem or poems he wished to discuss in class in the light of what we had been studying. One boy mentioned to me on the library steps one day that he had located some good ones. I said, "Fine. Who is the poet?"

"Paul Laurence Dunbar is his name."

"Good. Choose one or two and bring them to class," I said.

Shortly afterward he overtook me on the campus; he seemed hesitant and embarrassed. "Hey," he said. "You know what I found out? That Paul Laurence Dunbar is a Negro."

"Well?" I said. And then, since he made no response, "Surely that doesn't matter."

"Oh," he said. "No. I guess not." But it did.

It happened that the news came on the car radio one

day as a Negro man was riding to the campus with me
so that he could take my car to be serviced. A sit-in resulting in violence was reported as having occurred in
Maryland or somewhere distant, and the Negro man remarked to me, "It looks like those people are just trying to
stir up trouble. They ought to leave well enough alone."
And I found myself arguing with a Negro that the situation of the Negro demanded at least some kind of action
beyond leaving "well enough" alone.

In the spring of 1963 I attended the Southern Literary
Festival in Jackson, Mississippi. The Festival has been
traditionally segregated, its members being largely segregated white Southern schools (a fact which received considerable attention at the 1964 session when Stephen
Spender, Walter Allen, and John Gassner refused to appear for that reason), but at the opening session, featuring
Eudora Welty, several Negro college students walked in
and sat near the front of the large, crowded auditorium.
There was no fuss or flurry at all, and the only remark I
heard expressing any significant individual disturbance
over the fact was from a very privately "liberal" professor
who said with a nervous laugh that he had really not
known what to do when they came right in and sat down
not far from him.

Later, at another session of the Festival, Shelby Foote
received a sustained ovation in the same auditorium when,
at the conclusion of an excellent, perceptive speech on
William Faulkner, he remarked that Ross Barnett was not
the first Snopes to live in the governor's mansion.

When I first went to Louisiana I had a very interesting
class in which there was a very bright, very conservative
young man with whom I enjoyed brief debates. Shortly
before I left Louisiana in the summer of 1963 I saw the

young man a couple of times and had some pleasant conversations. During the last of these I asked if I had not seen a Goldwater sticker on his car. He said yes, and asked who I was for.

"Kennedy," I told him.

He looked at me a moment and said, "Really?" He had known before that I had favored Kennedy very strongly against Nixon, but I suppose he had forgotten. It was almost as startling there to hear an open good word for Kennedy as for integration.

"Sure," I said. "And give me enough time and I'll convince you." I was continuing the half-serious banter we had carried on nearly two years before.

"It would take a long time," he replied.

"About three days. We'd have to start from the roots."

He laughed, and then he said, "No, I know I shouldn't let racial feelings influence me this way, but I can't seem to help it."

Not long ago I was talking with a friend of the family who has been all my life like an uncle to me. He asked me how my father was doing now that he was retired, and I told him that Dad was raising tomatoes up to four pounds each, working harder in the garden in one day than I could in a week, and that he was really enjoying a new experience: teaching. That career he started at about seventy-five, and it really made him light up just to talk about it.

"Where is he teaching?"

"At a Negro seminary," I told him.

"Fine," my friend said. "That's an excellent thing. Why, if I had a million dollars, I don't know how I could spend it better than to help them educate their own people for their own churches and schools."

VIII

Where the War Was

FIREWORKS go with Christmas in my mind; when I was a boy we celebrated the birth of Christ rather than the Fourth of July with sparklers and roman candles and firecrackers. It never occurred to me to wonder why, because for years I was unaware that the rest of the country was backward. Since then I have been told that Mississippi did not celebrate the Fourth like the other states because it was on the Fourth of July in 1863 that Vicksburg fell.

The town of Vicksburg bears two minor resemblances to San Francisco: some of its streets are very steep and it has no room to spread out. San Francisco has the ocean and the bay on three sides. Vicksburg has the Mississippi River on one side and is hemmed in elsewhere by the battle lines and trenches of the long siege of 1863, presently the site of a national park.

The Civil War itself is kept alive at Vicksburg now most

vividly by the federal government. Through the years it has been fascinating to me to drive through the green lawn of the battlefield and look at the various monuments erected by the states in honor of their dead. The Illinois monument was a favorite of ours; within its high, topless dome each slightest whisper becomes the drawn-out hiss of a lingering echo. The decaying lookout towers, built so that tourists could view the rolling hills and their entrenchments, were a source of joy and terror to us. Circular concrete stairs wound up through several railed concrete platforms, narrower and narrower the higher we climbed. Most of our interest in the park had no conscious bearing on the battle fought there, though the presence of towers and monuments kept the fact alive in our minds, and in later years our interest shifted to following at least cursorily the lines of battle, sighting over an escarpment at what the Tennessee troops must have seen, or, in the other direction, perhaps a detachment from Wisconsin.

Fort Hill, though, fascinated us doubly from the very first. From its high bluff the town is visible, the wide Mississippi coming down under the bridge and curving westward, the influx of the Yazoo, the flat, flat land of Louisiana. Cannons stand in the small declivity, overlooking the river and the countryside. It is impossible for a boy not to climb on the cannons, and not to play war, running at a crouch from gun to gun and dodging the imagined fire of the enemy.

Below is a graveyard of crosses among moss-hung live oak trees, cool and silent and, to a child, ancient.

World War I seemed centuries away, when we were very young, although some of its shell-shocked victims wandered the streets of Jackson, and our parents talked of it as yesterday. The Civil War was, of course, virtually contemporary in our minds with the Spanish-American War, the War of 1812, and the Revolution, all of which were associated with the first Thanksgiving.

But there was a significant difference, even before age and schooling spread things out for us somewhat. The Civil War was fought on our ground. Indians had been there, too, because we could find their arrowheads which had weathered into the ground and out again. The old chapel had been, they told us, hospital and stable; we could see it there — the same physical presence. Where the Clinton city hall stands there had been a small frame building Grant had used as headquarters. I saw a picture of it. The Civil War we tied in with the Revolution dimly, but still locally, because of a picture in an old college year-book of the carriage Lafayette rode in when he made his triumphant visit to the United States in the 1820's. Out from Clinton we could locate the vague remnants of Governor Leake's old home, where the carriage had stood.

But the most vivid physical evidence of the war on our own soil was in the gray-coated minié balls we would find, sometimes misshapen and sometimes unmarred, in the same way we found the arrowheads. The gray oxided metal cool to the touch and heavy in the hand was reality, and the war which had been held unwittingly at such a distance would tighten in to us, go along with us as a minié ball with the marbles in a pants pocket.

When my father was an evangelist, I used to go with him to a revival meeting every summer. I believe that it was on one of these trips that we went together to the home of a very old man who had been a Confederate soldier. We sat with him in the backyard, which I recall as having a shade tree and a grapevine and much bright sunlight, and listened as he told about his experiences in the war. I remember more clearly than his story my father's turning to me and saying, "Listen to this; this is history, and soon you won't be able to hear a firsthand account." I seem to remember that the man's account included either a retreat or an escape, and his living off the countryside, perhaps wounded, as he made his way home. I cannot remember at all what the man looked like, although I believe he carried a cane.

A good portion of my life has centered around what is always referred to as the Historic Old Chapel on the campus of Mississippi College. In front of it each year a Confederate reunion was held, probably sponsored by the United Daughters of the Confederacy; at least some of the ladies of the town seemed to be in charge. Our rather ragtag troop of Boy Scouts was sometimes called upon to help, but I believe that my mother took us even before I was old enough for Scouts.

It was shady and cool under the elm trees, and the tall white columns, flanked by a few old cedars, rose high above us. One man, an officer in uniform, I can recall vividly as he stood beside a walk near the central drinking fountain, which even then had ceased to work. He was still very straight and military, and when someone remarked on the fact, he showed with a cane how when he was a military cadet at, perhaps, Virginia Military Institute or West Point, he had been made to hold a broomstick tightly against his back in the bend of his elbows; thus he had developed the habit of military bearing so thoroughly he had never lost it through the nearly seventy years it must have been since the war.

The ladies served coffee, but one old man caused a flurry of excitement by refusing to drink it unless they served it to him in a tin cup. He had learned to drink coffee from a tin cup in the war, and he would never touch it any other way. It may have been this same veteran who gathered a group of us Scouts about him by the force of his stories and showed us with his walking cane how he used to shoot Yankees, and told us how he could take on any ten Yankees any time. It happened that one of the few boys who owned a uniform had moved in from somewhere in the North and was known as "Yankee." Yankee stood with some others behind the old man, and so finally one of us said, "Well, there's a Yankee behind you right now," and the old man looked slowly around, apparently as nonplussed as Yankee, a blond, good-looking boy, who blushed scarlet and made us think maybe he wasn't quite so tough as we had always considered him.

My great-grandfather and one or more of my great-uncles had been in the war, and there was some story of an escape and about the loyalty of an ex-slave who eventually was buried just outside the family cemetery, and then later the fence was moved to include him with the master he had served so faithfully even in the war. The cemetery I remember in Standing Pine, however, and where my grandparents are buried, is not very far down the red clay road from the old homeplace, away from town.

We used to walk there with my grandmother every time we visited her. An unpainted barn faced the house alongside the road. It was surrounded by bitterweeds, and beyond it, past a few small pines and down the pasture hill a little way in the sparse grass, were the eroded gullies down the slick sides of which we all slid one long-ago wet Sunday when the grandchildren were together, ruining our Sunday clothes and setting off a string of spankings. On the opposite side of the road a small unpainted house with wooden shingles squatted exposed in bare dirt; behind it was a cotton field, and beside it a road branched off to Standing Pine Creek and the swimming hole near which I once watched some men seine a barrow pit and haul in an illegal bass along with the catfish.

Not far past the junction with the side road was the cemetery. First we would see a thin line of very tall, bare-trunked pines which stood just beyond the small plot of graves. The cemetery itself changed in appearance over the years as my grandmother with some help from a few neighbors put in hours and hours of work weeding and planting so that my grandfather would lie in a place of some beauty and dignity at least until she joined him.

Toward the back of the cemetery was a grave which lay north and south instead of east and west like all the others. We were told that it was the grave of a deserter (presumably in the Civil War, although my impression may have been wrong) who had hidden out at home. He was captured, taken to the cemetery, and shot at the edge of a grave designed to perpetuate his disgrace and, it seems, to make it at least awkward to rise up with the saints on the last day.

IX

Lost in the Gray

THE CIVIL WAR and the hardships and indignities of
Reconstruction were still significant currents in the South
when I grew up, but they most often ran beneath the surface. Sometimes a sudden energetic little spring would
surprise us, and occasionally we would happen upon a
stream that we had to walk along for some distance before
finding a place to wade across, but generally our land, for
all its minié balls, was much like the rest of the country.

We were taught "Northern" history back then, before
the textbooks were purged, and we looked back patrioti-
cally to the Pilgrims as our Fathers, to George Washington
and Abraham Lincoln as our greatest Presidents, and to
the freeing of the slaves as a milestone of humanitarian
accomplishment. The central legend of America was ours;
such a thing as two lines of development, one from Massa-
chusetts and the other from the Jamestown colony, diverg-
ing to form separate cultures economically and spiritually

antithetical to each other — such an interpretation of history never intruded into our dreams. The Civil War was real; the evidence was all around us. But it was a Romance acted out. Reconstruction was the name of a nightmare nobody dared tell before breakfast for fear it would come true.

Perhaps the most noteworthy symptom was defensiveness. I remember my own superior amusement when the little brother of a girl in our high school crowd didn't realize that "Yank" and "Yankee" were commonly used to designate all Americans, including Mississippians. It was just as World War II drew us in; a group of us were briefly in the apartment of the girl, after Prayer Meeting one Wednesday night, and we paused to hear the new war song being introduced on the radio by Eddie Cantor.

The song was called, "We Did It Before and We Can Do It Again." When somewhere along in it the lyrics indicated something about the Yanks being invincible, though in simpler words, the little brother shocked us all by jumping up from the floor to declare that any Southerner could outfight any ten Yankees any time.

Few Mississippi people had so naïve an approach to the language, but defensiveness was just under the surface all the time. Earlier I had heard considerable criticism of a professor at the college because a picture he had taken appeared in a textbook history of the South. It was of the dark old grocery store in the middle of town, with its tin awning and peeling posters. The publishers had included also a streamlined new service station in Jackson to show the two sides of the emerging South, but local people felt that the professor had betrayed us all. The picture gave a wrong impression of Clinton, and pictures like that did us no good.

One of the most persistent feelings of persecution in the

South was related to radio. People were accustomed to hearing "standard" American (or radio American) spoken on the air, and so whenever a Southern voice came slurring in among the regular cadences it hung out like a sore tongue. Of course the Southern dialect was an easy laugh on the comedy shows, and generally was about as genuine as a stage Irishman. "Honey chile" was a slab of Dixie talk that most of us never heard in real life, and the old comic bit of saying "Y'all" to one person would leave a good Mississippian red-faced and slowly speechless. I did once hear "Y'all" addressed to one person, me, by a Negro waiter in Birmingham in 1948. I'll never forget it.

Anyhow, as some of us began to discover from home recorders, we do sound somewhat that way. When in 1949 or 1950 the motion picture made from William Faulkner's *Intruder in the Dust* was released, my friend and I teaching the veterans' night school decided the movie should be good Mississippiana and might have some claims on a literature class, and so we took the students down the street to see it. He and I enjoyed the movie very much; it didn't occur to us that somehow we should resent it. But one of the students was quite irritated when we arrived at the schoolhouse afterward. What incensed him was the way that the Mississippi people were depicted as talking. His leading declaration was, "I ain't never *heerd* anybody talk like that!"

One of my friends who was at Ole Miss at the time and watched the filming around Oxford was also indignant. He said that the movie people dubbed in voices for the local residents who appeared in brief speaking roles, to make them sound worse. I was in Oxford the following year, however, and the people he had mentioned to me sounded by then just as they had on the movie sound track.

Faulkner himself was hardly appreciated by most people in Mississippi. One principal reason was that, like the picture of the dark old grocery store, his fiction was not of the tone, spirit, and general intellectual level of a Chamber of Commerce brochure. It was not only Mississippians who thought Faulkner was depicting the South as a land of illiterates and degenerates; a great many literary and social critics did too — and believed the picture they thought he was giving. In the thirties he was often classified as another Erskine Caldwell, and even Caldwell was not given his due. Actually, Faulkner's account of Mississippi is so accurate and so nearly complete that the temptation is to say to those curious about the state, simply, "Read Faulkner." But his is not a literal picture; that is, the literal element is often true to its specific locale and conditions, all right, but the deep sources of motive are true far beyond the characters in, say, *As I Lay Dying,* so that they illuminate both Mississippi and the age-old world.

As I was saying, however, local people resented Faulkner's "picture" of Mississippi. When I taught in the high school in Oxford in 1953–55, I discovered in my ninth- and tenth-grade classes a real animosity toward Faulkner. Of course, these students had not read any of his works, and, some of them declared, never would. The antagonism was adopted from their parents, many of whom had never read Faulkner either. I despaired of argument, and finally one day I read to each of the various classes a very moving and very funny short story called "Two Soldiers." All of them loved it, and they talked about it enthusiastically. Finally in each class one student would say, "Who wrote it?" I would answer, "William Faulkner." There would be a stunned silence, and then somebody would say, "Well, I didn't know he wrote anything like that." And in general the kids left Faulkner alone afterwards, at least in my presence.

It was not altogether the feeling that we were being ridiculed by outsiders that made the North so useful a tool for politicians of the Theodore G. "The Man" Bilbo's stripe, but since most of our memory and legend of outrageous mistreatment during the postwar years, and our various forms of mistrust arising from discriminatory freight rates and Northern journalistic hauteur, and our envy of the prosperity evidenced in magazine advertisements and in radio comedies whose conflict turned on whether to spend the vacation at the beach or in the mountains — since all of these things occupied one basic lair in the bowels of the Southerner, the whole mass of irritations would come roaring out as one at a taunting word or a patronizing tone of voice from the North.

Bilbo and others did use the North's equally touchy sensibility to keep in power, and by continuing in power keep that sensibility raw for the next easy employment. The Southern demagogue would harangue a little gathering with some patently foolish platform, known to be ridiculous and taken by most Mississippi voters as the only available vaudeville. "And as for the niggers," he would shout, "what we ought to do is send them all back to Africa." The crowd would cheer. The Northern newspapers would take it, or pretend to take it, seriously; I have wondered how many of them were in the game of improving the circulation in the same way that Bilbo was in the game of getting a large enough share of the votes to retain his position as "second most useless" Senator in Washington.

In any case, the papers would express great horror, and Bilbo or his like would then call attention to the attack of the Northern press upon himself, and say, "Look at that! *They* know who to attack! You see who it is they are afraid of! The Northern press is out to beat me, and we're not going to let them cram that down our throats, are we!" And by God we didn't let them.

Many Southerners were quite conscious of the whole interaction, of course, which is the only reason I noticed it at all growing up: I heard a great deal of talk about it. However, if one of us did not happen to have such things called to his attention, he was likely to have an incredible sort of blindness on the North-South issue. One good friend of mine was in just such a spot, and some of us caused him considerable distress by playing on his weakness, partly, I say in my own defense, in order to try to help him out of it.

We had been friends for years before World War II, and we, along with many reservists at our college, were called into active duty in the Navy and sent right back to the same college. There we lived alongside other young Navy collegians from many other states, notably Iowa and Nebraska. I don't suppose I had ever really noticed until that time that my friend could not think clearly at all if Negroes or the North were the topic of conversation. It became apparent, though, when another old acquaintance used deliberately to talk to me in his presence about how much prettier Negro girls were than white girls, until our friend would explode from his bunk and have to be subdued.

That bit of boyish fun was just to warm up for later in the day, however. At noon we marched to the chow hall (formerly and subsequently the cafeteria) where we always sat opposite our neighbors from the North; our sensitive friend was genuinely very fond of these Midwesterners and considered them excellent people and the

best of buddies. And so the meal would start off pleasantly enough with general abusive banter, and it would
go along with cornfed heartiness until one of us would
slyly introduce a North-South element into the conversation. Soon there would be a discussion of the merits of
the regions: the manliness of the men, attractiveness of
the girls, richness of the soil, tastiness of the hamburgers,
or whatever. We boys from the South would keep the
argument going, work it up to a fine pitch, and then ease
gradually over to the Northern side, so that only our friend
would remain defending his beloved Southland. It would
not be long before the strain of his lone stand, and perhaps
a just feeling of having been betrayed, would begin to
tell, and soon he would be trying to force all six or seven
of us outside to fight.

At that we would all begin equivocating and rather
swiftly work our way around to an accommodation with
his viewpoint; his face would subside from purple to red,
and he would leave the chow hall friends. Until the next
noon. If he ever saw through our perfidy he was gentle-
man enough never to accost us with it.

Another Southerner I knew in the Navy seemed to live
in order to sweat and bray like an Arkansas mule.

When Arkie traveled with four of us by rail from Oakland, California, to Jacksonville, Florida, by way of Chicago, he began before we got on the train — in an Oakland
liquor store, shouting his way through the intricate job of
buying something to drink on the trip. He let us and the
general neighborhood know how he liked to drink down
in Arkansas, and then read from bottles specifically what
he liked to drink. Finally he found a label that really
excited him.

"Man, here it is! You see that? That's some of that

Southern Comfort. Ah mean, that's the real good old drink
down in Arkansas, man. Ah just guzzle it down!" He
bought a fifth of it. Some of the others got bottles of
other things — I did not drink, and so I paid little
attention.

There is hardly a doubt in my mind that Arkie was in
reality on a par with me in ignorance of alcohol, and that
he had neither tasted nor heard of Southern Comfort
before that time. But we heard of it constantly afterward.
I have visions of the dry wasteland, the dead stubble
with mountains in the distance, sliding interminably by
outside while Arkie filled the railroad car with shouts
about how he was from the South and how he loved that
Southern Comfort. He tried to get other people to drink
some, too, but nobody ever took more than a taste. I did
not know at the time that Southern Comfort is a cherry-
flavored liqueur, thick and sweet, and hardly the thing to
be drunk straight out of the bottle like wine. Eventually
Arkie disappeared, and soon we could hear him in the
men's room noisily repudiating his favorite drink.

I'm afraid it gave us some malicious pleasure. I was
from the South, and defensive enough about it, too, I'm
sure, but Arkie embarrassed me. I even enjoyed with
malice the next thing that happened to him, although I
think that even then I must have known it was in a way
both significant and sad. In Chicago a big labor convention was going on, and we wound up in the party of a
huge Irish labor leader with a few older people and two
very pretty girls.

Since I was not drinking, the Irishman asked me to keep
an eye on the girls, because they were nice girls and
worked for a good friend of his, and he didn't want anything happening to them. The young ladies were perfectly

safe, although they were deservedly popular. Arkie, among others, was taken with them and in his incredibly obvious way desired some response, however minute. Eventually, when the girls were seated on a bed and the Irishman and others were seated on the floor, singing "Bellbottom Trousers," Arkie moved in and sat near one of the girls. Cautiously, Arkie lay down so that his head was in the girl's lap and then he tentatively relaxed. The girl paid no attention to him at all; she kept right on singing. But the big Irishman had been watching; he winked at me and surreptitiously eased one of his huge hands up to Arkie's head and ran his fingers through Arkie's hair. Such a smile of absolute bliss! This, he seemed to sigh, was what he had meant all along by Southern Comfort.

X

Here and There

THE DISCOMFORT of Southerners in the North, where they must be subjected to de facto integration, may seem to be inevitable, but experience does not really bear out the expectation. Some Southerners, true, are terribly uncomfortable in the North; I can recall several moments of something akin to agony a friend of mine went through in Chicago not long after the war, but they were caused by the lack of politeness, the simple bluntness, of the city folk, and his skin had not been calloused by hard usage. When I had just returned to Mississippi some ten years later, another friend almost sent me flying back as far north as Kentucky by recounting to me his adventure of having to be in the North for a short while, and by telling me as he stood there shivering as if with a chill how he *had* to get back home. The pathological necessity for being home, in the nest, was what frightened me; it may be latent in all of us.

But in practice many Southerners adjust very easily to
the North. When we lived for the summer of 1953 in
Willow Run Village in Michigan, while I attended the
University, the fact of Alabama white people living there
next to Southern Negroes in the federal housing apartments seemed to me likely to cause some difficulties.
However, in every such case I knew of, the families were
neighborly and apparently at ease. As an ardent and
vociferous segregationist is said to have replied when it
was discovered that the college he taught in for a year
in the West was integrated, and that he had sat in the
grill where some Negroes were also sitting, "Well, that's
different. That's not here."

However, there were few Negroes living next to white
people at Willow Run. Integration was token there, too.
Among the white apartments Negro families would be
scattered, one here and one away over there, but beyond
a little hill there was another spread of apartments — out
the back, so to speak — and these were all Negro, so far
as I was ever able to determine. The federal government
had its own Niggertown in Michigan.

Many of the Southern white people went back South
and right back into the segregated society, even more
convinced, since they saw too that all the righteousness
they had resented all this time in the North was hypocriti-
cal; "At least," they thought, and many have been saying
recently, "we don't lie about it; we're honest."

Another sort of fruitless meeting between North and
South has come about when the Northerner moves down
to Dixie. Quite often what seems to happen is that he
comes in with the feeling that he will be forced to endure
this benighted place, and ends by adopting its outlook.
Often he comes with no broader view than the Southerner,

and no better brains. One case was notorious in a small town where we lived for a while. A woman with a very high degree of education moved with her family into the town, which was perhaps 70 percent Negro and not by any means a wealthy area, and swore immediately and publicly that she would not rest until every Negro in that town lived in as good a house as she did. That was some time before our arrival there, and it was said that she had ceased talking about it, although no Negroes and very few white people lived in as good a house as she did.

We have run into various minor situations which illuminate the basic similarities of the attitudes of people all over. At a very liberal gathering in the North some few years ago, we spent much of our time answering questions about how it was in Mississippi. Sometimes the questions were virtually accusations; often they were more immediately sympathetic than we found comfortable.

At luncheon one day we sat with a couple from the West; they queried us for a few minutes, and then for some reason confided to us in hushed tones that there was a mixed couple, of course, in our midst. Well, neither my wife nor I have been sufficiently removed from our upbringing to be around a mixed couple and not even notice, and so we were immediately puzzled: we had seen no mixed couple at all. "Are you sure?" we said. They were, and they identified the couple for us. Of course, it was not a mixed couple at all. It was an Oriental married to an Occidental. Apparently it was all in what color one was brought up blind to.

It is seldom given Mississippians to feel righteous in the outside world, and believe me the temptation that day was strong.

Most people are aware now, as apparently not many

years ago few were, that the race problem is not just Southern. Our year in the West during 1960–61 would have made this very clear to us if we had not been aware of it already. I think of one particular conversation that epitomizes the whole affair to me, partly because the man I was talking with has my genuine liking and admiration. We had discussed the situation in the South for some quarter hour when he said to me. "Well, we're beginning to have our problems with them, too." And I was too polite to respond, "And we're going to as long as we think in terms of 'we' and 'our' and 'them.' "

There was a severe problem of communication with many of my inquisitors during that year. I decided later that one reason they insisted on telling me to my face that Mississippians are per se stupid and evil was that they considered that I was not in the slightest representative of Mississippi; surely that must have been it. On the other hand, some of them were capable of considering themselves as completely representative of their home area, so that I was invited to picture New York or Indiana as states of complete benevolence and culture, occupied exclusively by Ph.D.'s.

Again one conversation stands out for me, largely because I pursued it to the bitter end. My interrogator was a graduate student of advanced standing, from New York. He began by asking me how I could stand to live in Mississippi. I tried to tell him that, aside from certain moral and legal questions which were extremely easy to ignore, Mississippi was a very comfortable place to live. One by one I met his objections: I told him that we did live in quite comfortable houses which were most often, at his social and economic level, air conditioned; people drove good cars, also often air conditioned; the race problems were kept so quiet that it took a real effort even to discover that they existed; the people were neighborly and pleasant; in short, it was comfortable.

"But you have no culture at all there," he protested. I tried to tell him that, of course, there was a very clearly defined culture there, which made it all the easier to live in comfort, assuming that was one's desire. But that if he meant cultural activities, it was true that they were fewer than in San Francisco, say, but that I found that I was unable and unwilling to take advantage of all that were offered in Mississippi, and being as near as we were to San Francisco at the time, I found that I had neither the money, the time, nor the real interest to take anywhere near full advantage of them. Did he?

"Well," he replied, "you don't have any big league baseball down there."

(And Ross Barnett would have countered, I'm sure, "Yes, my friend, but we have a football team at Ole Miss that's always one of the finest in the country, and we had two Miss America's in a row. Come see us!")

Of course, that conversation was not typical; it just makes the typical horribly obvious. And I did have a great deal of sympathy with what the young man was trying to get at. The problem was, he wanted it simple. It's very hard to have to learn that a man or a society does not have to scowl and scowl to be a villain.

After a couple of years in Louisiana, we invaded the North and West again. At one meeting in 1963 a number of Negro participants gave moving accounts of their own experiences and feelings. One family had driven up to Michigan from Texas, trying again and again all the way up to and into Michigan to find a decent place to sleep, and being turned away again and again. Such an account could have been given at any earlier time, I suspect, but a couple of attitudes were new to me in their open expression, one that segregation was an integral part of American life, and it was impossible to eradicate it: the thing to do was to set up separate societies. (To which a Jewish man replied, "Haven't you learned anything from the history of my people?") And another that since people could not overcome prejudice without an effort, their attempts were not acceptable.

My point here is that there seemed at least to be much freer discussion on much less superficial elements of the racial situation than had existed three years before. This outside the South, of course.

I discovered in the West, too, a clearly different sort of attitude. Granted that many of the young people who were indignant about Mississippi had a kind of missionary fervor that only the young are likely to sustain, it seemed to me to have much greater understanding and much more genuine compassion as its basis than had the simply superior attitude of three years before. One of their spokesmen cautioned them all not to think of Mississippi as foreign. It isn't foreign, he said; it is where an American disease has come to a head, so that we can see it. But the poison is in us all, and we must fight it in ourselves and in our own communities as well as there.

Apparently by now virtually everybody in the country is aware of what is thought of as either the Negro's problem or the Negro problem. A friend of mine in California speculated recently that the white liberal non-Southerner is less at ease in a social gathering with Negroes than is the Southern segregationist. Such a Southerner has the Negro thoroughly "placed" within his mind; he knows just how to act around him. But, my friend said, the white liberal non-Southerner, aware that he does not "know" the Negro, is always doubtful about how whatever he says or does may be taken. The segregationist will be sure of his rightness, free of any distressing insecurity, and so polite and quite sociable.

But in spite of the increasing understanding in the West of the Mississippi problem, and partly because of it, another element is more apparent. Many Western white people agree that the situation in Mississippi needs clearing up, but they will hedge around the proposition of having Negroes move into their own neighborhood. And many who will readily agree to allowing Negroes on their block will draw in noticeably at the mention of the possibility of racial intermarriage. Most of the latter prefer to talk about the motivations and desires of "the Negro" and leave themselves out of it.

I often recall a thing Eudora Welty said a few years ago in Jackson, Mississippi. The Little Theatre there had done *Cat on a Hot Tin Roof,* and a considerable stir had resulted. Apparently a reporter overheard a city official remark privately in the lobby that such plays should not be allowed on the stage, or some such. The reporter then blew it up into the possible closing of the play by the city — which seems never to have been considered — with a fair amount of resultant controversy pro and con. Later the Little Theatre produced *Visit to a Small Planet.*

At the workshop during the following summer Miss Welty appeared as the principal member of a panel, and she was asked by a young member of the *Visit* cast why it was that people had castigated as immoral Tennessee Williams's play, which attempted a moral position on sex, whereas they had casually accepted Gore Vidal's play, which had used illicit sex for laughs in a situation which could hardly be funny from a "moral" position.

Miss Welty replied that when the unpleasant truth is put before our eyes, we have various devices for refusing to see it. "Down here," she said, "we say, 'Well! I've never seen anybody like her in my whole life!' But up East they say, 'I know exactly what her trouble is.'"

XI

Jumping from Conclusions

THERE'S AN OLD SAYING that the largest cities in Mississippi are Memphis and New Orleans. Even now Jackson, by far the largest within the state boundaries, claims only about 150,000 people. It is no giant metropolis; but it was for us growing up, and is still to everybody within driving distance, the City. Even when it contained fewer than 50,000 people Jackson seemed large and crowded to me, and I can recall most vividly the ride home from downtown: between stores and banks and movie theaters and cafes and hotels, under the Illinois Central tracks, past a few more stores and the Coca-Cola plant which had been a church, alongside a little park, the Masonic hall, the large Calvary Baptist Church, the zoo and Livingston Park with a big lake for swimming, on out broad West Capitol with streetcar tracks down the middle and nice homes on each side and watermelon-red crape myrtle bordering the street. Then the overhead bridge, a high steel structure just at the city limits. From the top you could look down on the trains it was built to avoid and on a cattle farm with a huge barn. When we dropped down the slope of the bridge out of the city, alongside thick oak woods, suddenly it was cool and natural again, and we would know even with our eyes closed that we were not very far from home.

Two and a half miles from home it was to Jackson's city limits, and the same distance from home to Clinton. Though close in, Clinton was not a suburb, as it may be considered by many people now; it was its own town. Of course now, too, the city limits of both have reached farther and farther out so that they almost touch. And although back then there were many houses along our "street" (Highway 80 it was), few white people lived as far as a block off the main road, whereas now most of the backwoods is honeycombed with streets and good middle-class-white homes.

I learned to drive on a back road which cut off the highway a mile toward Jackson. It was gravel and little-used, and we would take it as the first of a number of unpaved roads on the way to pick blackberries in the woods and pasture around my great-aunt's house — the real "country." The little country church they went to, and which seemed to me so far out it was hard to find, is now a large metropolitan church well within the city. The country is — somewhere else.

Jackson has always been a clean and pleasant city, with no coal smoke or whatever to soil the buildings, which reach at the tallest more than twenty stories high. People used to speak to each other on the streets, and although we distrusted the few hard-looking boys at pool room entrances, we thought that if we had to live in a city, we'd take Jackson. For cleanliness and friendliness, if you're of the right group of people it still would be among the most pleasant of places to live.

It was very easy to go into Jackson and see the clean skyline, the pleasant stores, the red crape myrtles, and not be aware of any other aspect of the city. But we would now and then visit a mill, not far off Capitol Street, for cottonseed hulls and cottonseed meal to feed our two cows, and on the way we would drive between Negro shacks. Or where Farish Street crosses Capitol, we would glance down Farish at the small Negro shops and their crowds which cut a black line of poverty across the white city. Negroes shopped in the rest of town, of course, but most ten cent stores were conveniently near Farish Street, and the more exclusive department stores were farther up toward the Old Capitol, which had stood at the head of Capitol Street since before the Civil War.

Part of my morning as a boy was the Jackson *Clarion-Ledger*, which helped form my taste in comics, if nothing else. And when we were in Jackson in the afternoon we would hear a newsboy's chant, "Jackson DAILY *News* E'ENIN' paper." The *Clarion-Ledger* was considered a good, solid, moral, responsible newspaper. The *Daily News* featured the inspired journalistic vituperation of its longtime editor Major Fred Sullens. His column was not considered "nice," though many people read it avidly and enjoyed it. I remember talk of his having called Bilbo a pusillanimous old buzzard, and it was said that his opposition to a candidate insured that candidate's victory. When Paul Johnson, the father of the present governor, had finally been elected governor, he happened upon Fred Sullens in the lobby of the Walthall Hotel one day and caned him.

Sullens' rhetoric made his writing interesting, but the *Clarion-Ledger* was mostly just safe. When the *C-L* built

a new building some years ago and was moving in, some of
the reporters said that there should be a symbol above the
door, and they suggested a man shrugging his shoulders.
The editorial policy was characterized as "against sin and
for preachers."

Now the two papers are owned by the same publishers.
According to accounts at the time, the *Clarion-Ledger*
owners began secretly buying stock in the rival paper; Sullens discovered it, went to court and won, but he was too
far gone financially as a result to refuse to sell the paper to
the publishers of the *Clarion-Ledger*. He was hired as editor and given a free hand. After the switch, Sullens called
his staff together and said that some of them might think
he had prostituted himself, taking the editorship in such
circumstances. "But if so," he is reputed to have said,
"I'm the highest paid he-whore in the state of Mississippi."

Partly because of advertising rates in the two papers,
another afternoon daily was begun in competition. The
State Times had a more intelligent, more courageous, and
generally saner editorial policy than the established papers, but after several years it folded and its assets, too,
were bought out by the *Clarion-Ledger–Daily News*. The
only other white newspaper I know of (and I am ignorant
of the Negro press there) is a small "area" paper, *The*
Northside Reporter, put out by Pulitzer Prize winner
Hazel Brannon Smith; it was bombed during the 1964
Democratic National Convention, apparently because all
these years in Lexington and Durant, where she owns
weekly papers, Hazel has been honest and fearless in the
face of economic sanctions and physical threats.

The safer way to run a newspaper is to cater to the
popular causes and be careful to spell the names right in
the society pages and in the obituaries. Far out beyond
the last homes of my boyhood days, north of town, a very

rich new area opened up a few years ago. Eastover Drive became *the* address, and we used to drive through now and then to see the large homes as they were completed, and to read from signs, if we chose, the names of people whose houses were under construction. The death of one very wealthy man rated a very long and prominent *Clarion-Ledger* obituary which concluded with the statement that he had lived on Blank Boulevard, but he had planned to move soon to Eastover Drive.

The values, expressed and assumed, seem to be different from those of my boyhood in Mississippi, although partly because I was largely unaware of society and the possibility of climbing, then. In our branch of the family the good old virtue of "not puttin' on" was very strong, as it was with many people around us. But some things have made a change, and I see in the particular kind of change (or in the particulars which have belatedly become apparent to me) some principles of belief and of approach to "the truth" which are of great importance in understanding the plight of Mississippi today.

The kind of change and the rapidity and subtlety of its effect struck me a few years ago in church. In that same church I had, as a small boy, heard much discussion of the deadening ritual of more formal, less "genuine" churches; at that time a printed Sunday morning order of service was not distributed, partly for fear of its becoming set and ritualistic. But one Sunday some twenty-odd years later, the current pastor told us that we should love our Baptist brethren in South America in spite of our differences. Some of their churches there, he said, even sing the Doxology at the end of the service instead of at offering time.

"Our way of life," obviously, was not always honored in South America in this particular; but it was honored at

home with what seemed to me, though apparently to few
others, too great insistence and too incredible attempts
(no doubt honest in motive) at justification. A sermon
was preached, for instance, in the Baptist church which
earlier had instilled in me a firm belief in the freedom of
the individual, which drew two lessons from the march of
Joshua and his people around the doomed walls of Jericho:
(1) "Follow your leaders and be silent," and (2) "Regi-
mentation is a good thing."

When, in conversation with a longtime member of the
church, I voiced some objection to the sermon (does regi-
mentation bring walls tumbling *down*?), the loyal member
replied that those statements surely had not been made.
I established as well as I could that they had indeed been
made, and it was responded that, of course, the preacher
hadn't meant it that way.

Of course the preacher had meant it that way, and
eventually the person I had talked to inadvertently discovered that he also acted with devastating effect upon
the principle — no doubt believing he was right all the
time, and apparently disturbing scarcely at all the Baptist-
democrats who listened to him and worked along with
him. The sermon and the action blended quite easily
into the pattern of everyday comfort in traditional forms
which Mississippians enjoy and which thought and self-
examination might disrupt.

Or another sermon — not to belabor the ministry, but
largely because they are the only people who are forced
by the simple arrival of Sunday to stand up in public and
say something vaguely related to the ideas humans have
considered important for all the centuries of our history.
This one was a sermon on God and mammon and the idea
that no man can serve both. The reasoning was routed by
way of laying up treasures in heaven where moth and rust

do not corrupt nor thieves break in and steal, for "Where your treasure is, there will your heart be also." Here it double-clutched in mid-concept and went with appalling smoothness into a kind of reverse, with treasure, even the "in heaven" kind, identified of course as money, so that the meaning regressed into, "Where your money is, there will your heart be also," and therefore we can tell whether a man is a Christian or not by whether he puts his money into this church; and therefore, further, as an acting principle we should translate everything into money terms so that we can evaluate it.

Whoever cannot follow that reasoning might as well not try to talk about race to white Mississippians; the pattern is the same, whether for making God equal mammon or hate equal love.

Perhaps I should make it clear that I use Baptists, or misuse them, not because they are greater offenders than others, but because I know them better, I consider it more nearly "polite" to criticize one's own in order to make a point than to criticize those with whom one is not connected, and I assume that the lesson will be taken not as occasion for ridicule, but as occasion for a new look at what each of us is and thinks and lives among. I am convinced that the same kind of reasoning is latent in everybody and permeates in varying concentrations virtually every institution in the world.

Another sermon, if I may, then, made me sit up for a few minutes in surprise because it seemed about to advocate action in the spirit of the Jesus who died for others rather than in the spirit of the deacons of the Local Church of the Pharisee who turn away Samaritans at the door. The sermon was on sacrifice, and sacrifice was urged upon us at length, in the abstract; but the longer it was urged, the narrower its limits grew. When twelve struck, what was meant by sacrifice was finally clear: every Christian should sacrifice of his time and money just enough to attend services at that church and support its budget.

I was told of an elderly minister who addressed a group of young ministers when it appeared that they might decide to come out for something like integrating the churches. The older minister stood and said, "Now, brethren, you must deal with your own consciences on this matter. But I just want to tell you where *I* stand. I stand exactly where Jesus stood — right in the middle of the road."

It is not by any means just preachers; a professor at a Southern university was asked, "What is the greatest social problem of the world today?" And he replied, "Well, I think we need more kinds of wholesome activities on our college campuses."

Another, a dean this time, at a large Southern university, apparently was disturbed at opposition in faculty meeting to including a course in the curriculum at the request of the state legislature. The dean arose and said, "Gentlemen, the state legislature has always granted us complete academic freedom here, and if we don't do what they want us to, they're going to take it away from us!"

Perhaps it is all a kind of backward thinking, starting from what we want the answer to be and setting up the steps accordingly. The resultant logic is out of kilter, and in practice the method results in so great a disparity between statement and fact as to border on insanity.

It may be a related sort of rationalization that can make some people believe, even during the Civil War Centennial, that, as a copyrighted poem in the *Clarion-Ledger* proclaimed, we Mississippians can lick the Yankees any time we try. It must be true that many of us would be perfectly willing to make exactly the same stupid error the second time, and come to grief with genuine surprise. After all, we *wanted* it to come out to suit us, and everybody knows we're *good*.

When I was a college student, the professors took turns speaking in chapel. One rabidly unreconstructed Rebel delivered a written address on God in history. He read in a monotone, eyes on his manuscript, left forefinger pointing rafterward at an angle just above his left ear and waggling back and forth from time to time for some incomprehensible sort of emphasis. He read for the twenty minutes allotted, and the bell rang. He looked up, startled, his finger suspended. "Well," he said finally, "we'll go on a few minutes longer." He read on for the next ten minutes until God was about to conquer Napoleon at Waterloo, and the bell rang for class. That, he knew, was the allowable limit for nonvisiting speakers, and so he reluctantly quit.

The chapel sessions rolled around through the faculty and eventually back to him. He placed his manuscript on the speaker's stand and said, "You may remember that last time I spoke I didn't get to finish my speech on God in history. So I thought we'd go back to it again this time."

He hoisted his finger and began reading — not with Napoleon, but at the beginning. When, after the mild shock of the first bell, he read on until the second bell, he had again with admirable consistency reached the battle of Waterloo.

Granted that it would be impossible to demonstrate anything at all to such a mentality, what about the lesser manifestations of the same removal from uncomfortable reality? There is, in addition to the structure of our logic, our tacit agreement not to criticize each other, not to air our dirty white linen in public. How can you tell a man the awful truth about himself and still be polite? It was

not a Mississippian in the comic strip forerunners of television commercials who used to inform his girl friend he
couldn't marry her because she had body odor.

During the Democratic convention of 1960 I filled in
for a vacationing state editor in Jackson, and I was unfortunately in a position to hear conversations, or one side
of them, carried on between Jackson and Los Angeles.
The party I heard made no effort to be secretive, and I'm
sure had no thought that his account of things sounded
strange to me. There was a convention fight, as I recall
it, over the civil rights plank to the platform; at any rate,
a group of Southerners was given time to express a minority view. One man spoke, limiting his argument to
"States Rights," then Governor Ross Barnett and Judge
Tom Brady of Mississippi spoke, linking "States Rights"
closely with racial issues. I disagreed with them in the
extreme, and I was not particularly pleased to have them
represent me, as a Mississippi citizen, in such terms.
Somewhat to my surprise, I found no one at all who had
been pleased. At the office I was told that the talk there
had been totally against Barnett and Brady as having been
a disgrace to Mississippi, except for one man who was
also a sort of unofficial adviser to Ross. It was he whom I
heard talking by phone to Ross in Los Angeles.

"Yes, Governor," he said, "the folks are behind you one
hundred percent. Yes, sir. They're all proud of the showing you made. They'll be out with a brass band to meet
you. Everybody's behind you in this."

Not one other good word had I heard. How was the
Governor to know what the truth was? But, then, when
Ross barred James Meredith so politely from Ole Miss, it
came true. Maybe the adviser was right all the time. All
the folks were behind Ross in this; they just hadn't realized it yet.

XII

It Rained All Night
the Day I Left,
the Weather It Was Dry

Perhaps it is true that in Mississippi the people may overwhelmingly favor a man or an idea without knowing it, or at least without saying so. A conspiracy of polite silence for the sake of racial segregation and white supremacy easily extends itself into nonracial matters, into the very structures of thought itself. Bland corporate hypocrisy is a natural result, as is the inability to focus on almost any problem directly or deal with it reasonably; and there is a constant threat, since reason is lacking, of gross injustice or simple force. Mississippi's liquor laws provide so obvious an illustration of pervasive hypocrisy that even the most disinterested summary runs the risk of being discounted as caricature.

Mississippi remains the only legally dry state in the Union. For those too far away from all remembrance of Prohibition to understand the term, perhaps it should be explained that "legally dry" does not mean that, as in

Camelot, laws have been passed against unseasonable rain. But it might as well. The state has local option on beer, but no other alcoholic beverages may legally be sold, bought, transported, or possessed within the state.

When I was a boy and we went huckleberry picking in the woods around Clinton, once we stumbled upon something more potent than fresh fruit: a keg of whiskey carelessly camouflaged with leaves. We left it there and, when we returned home, called the sheriff. Later we saw in the classified ads a notice that a keg of whiskey had been found; owner should call at the sheriff's office.

Perhaps it was a ruse to catch a half-witted bootlegger, or perhaps not. The thing is that in Mississippi it is impossible to judge.

All recent governors of the state have preached prohibition. The one who was apparently the only genuine teetotaler, personally, sent out armed raids to establishments selling whiskey in several rather distant counties, but seemed to think nothing of stopping by improvised bars at various get-togethers to chat with his drinking fellow politicians and the press, and the areas of the state where liquor was openly sold he bothered not at all.

Jackson itself is a very easy place in which to get whiskey; some places are not. From many delta cities the citizens are accustomed to an occasional drive to Memphis to stock up. One delta lady was preparing for a party a few years ago, and drove dutifully to Memphis to get the principal ingredients. But an intervening hill county had elected a sheriff who took the law seriously, and some deltan apparently disliked the lady enough to report her. When she came through the hill county on the way back from Memphis, she was arrested by a deputy sheriff who complained that she was considerably late and had inconvenienced him unduly.

The arrest was not popular in the lady's home town, and soon the local newspaper ran a front-page picture of the lady receiving a consolation television set from her Memphis liquor dealer.

But in Jackson there are normally fewer difficulties. If a Jacksonian can afford it, he may join one of the key clubs in local hostelries. The price of the key admits him and his guests to a veritable nightclub with bar. No effort is made, within the club's confines, to disguise the liquor, although even in private clubs or private homes the liquor is quite against the law. When complaints arose a few years ago, pushed by people who were suffering under Jackson's Sunday closing laws, which they considered too binding and which were actually being enforced, some of the club operators were fined, but the fines were negligible, and although there may have been a slowing down of operations, it was certainly brief. The usual arrests concerning alcohol arise out of disturbance of the peace in some way, and/or concern the poorer whites and the Negroes.

Across the Pearl River from Jackson in a notorious former swampland now building into a suburban industrial area, the operator of an illegal establishment told me some years ago that the sheriff at that time had gone into office with the intention of cleaning up the Gold Coast, as it was called. He was independently wealthy and he refused all bribes, but when he discovered that keeping the law was impossible, he had to settle for keeping order.

The sellers of whiskey tried to cooperate — less to keep from having to pay a $500 fine and have one of their Negro employees spend some time in jail than to avoid the sharper crackdowns which would eventually come from too much disturbance and violence. Years ago talk of murders in the Gold Coast was common.

But without joining a key club and without driving across the river, even, the Jacksonian can get his liquor with ease. And for a not exorbitant price. Standard brands, I mean, not wildcat, though that too can be found. When Oklahoma was about to vote wet and leave us alone with our prohibition laws, I was working on a Jackson newspaper on weekends, and a friend and I used to check periodically the wire stories from Oklahoma City on how difficult it was to buy whiskey and how high the price had gone. When a fifth of bourbon reached $9.50 and had to be purchased at an arranged clandestine meeting some distance from town, the thirsty legislature voted wet. Old Crow, handed out the back of a "drive-in" store, ran $5 the fifth in Jackson at the time.

And presumably that included a Mississippi state tax as well as the federal taxes, since Mississippi has what is called the Black Market tax on all whiskey sold within the state. The tax rolls are not available to law enforcement officers.

Perhaps it wouldn't matter anyway. In Vicksburg, just thirty-five miles from the state capitol, anyone who wants to can walk into any number of stores and choose whatever brand of whatever kind of beverage he happens to want from the open shelves. Or he can have a martini before dinner in the restaurant of his choice.

The teetotaling governor who promised enforcement of the prohibition laws sent troops to the opposite side of the state, ninety miles away, to raid beer joints said to be selling liquor on the sly; apparently he had never been to Vicksburg, or never heard of it. Or maybe he was just very much like the rest of the state on this point: if he found it necessary to be a hypocrite, he might as well do it to suit himself. There was some advantage to advocating prohibition, to raiding in certain areas, to keeping up the front; but why lose Vicksburg votes?

Of course, as Oklahoma demonstrated, the way to get rid of prohibition would be to enforce it; not too long after that lesson, when a local option bill was killed in the Mississippi legislature, some of the members advocated what was called the Bone Dry Bill. If we were going to continue with prohibition, they said, we should enforce it. Either get rid of it or have it, and quit the open hypocrisy that made a mockery of all law, all authority, all honesty, all decency. The Bone Dry Law would require local officers to enforce the law or be penalized.

But in conjunction with the bootleggers the prohibitionists killed the bill.

A few years ago in a delta town, located on what used to be a curve of the Mississippi River but was now abandoned to lakehood, there was a particular bootlegger whose story, as I heard it, was rather touching. He had grown up on a dirt farm not far away until he was in his teens. Then he realized that his family was stuck there, making too little every year to break the deadening cycle of poverty, and he wanted something better out of life. The only way he knew to make any real money was to sell whiskey, and so he left the farm and went into the business. He prospered. When I used to see him occasionally (although in recent times a stricter sheriff had been put into office) he was driving a Cadillac. He was said to be extremely wealthy, and everyone spoke of him with some awe and some envy, but he was not accepted by the nice people of the town.

His wife, however, was accepted and somewhat pitied and to a degree, too, envied. She was a pleasant-looking woman with wide innocent eyes, and she was a regular and faithful member of a local teetotaling church. One day she went to a Missionary meeting in Vicksburg with three other ladies of the church. On the way home they

stopped at a service station to buy a soft drink, and since
it was extremely hot they went inside. There to their great
shock the walls were lined with shelves and the shelves
were stacked with unabashed bottles of whiskey. The
ladies looked at each other in wide-eyed silence for a moment before the bootlegger's wife spoke. "Why, look at
that!" she said indignantly. "And my husband has to hide
his in the lake!"

Had the lady been as cultured as her associates, she
would not have made such a faux pas. We Mississippians
have generally learned to accept the fact that our state has
to hide its liquor in the tax rolls, and we make no fuss
about it. One law for those who cooperate, and another
law for those who question. One law for white, one law
for black. Just put one in the right pocket and the other
in the left pocket, and never let your right hand know
what goes on in your left.

In such circumstances, one cannot afford logic, or he
will chop off one hand by the action of the other. I have
been told that some members of the state legislature, carried away down the path of bills they were rapidly advocating in an effort to circumvent the law of the land, shot
onward to the logical conclusion and proposed with agi-
tated zeal that the state secede from the Union; but their
saner colleagues shushed them. Mustn't go that far, because the state could not exist without federal funds. Attack the federal government; utilize all your freedom of
speech and action to claim that the federal government
has taken away all your freedom of speech and action, so
that you can continue to pass laws taking away still further the freedom of your local citizens. But always keep
the proper hand within the proper pocket.

A couple of meetings I have attended over the years in
Mississippi represent to me not the average meeting, but

the epitome of virtually all meetings there. The experiences are of two basic kinds; one is the meeting which is really, though not ostensibly, controlled, and the other is the kind of meeting in which democracy is groping toward something it wants, but is hampered by facts and feelings at variance with each other.

The second kind occurred in a rural county, and the participants were teachers and administrators of the surrounding schools. Perhaps I should in all fairness say that the education of the white children in most of Mississippi is reasonably comparable with that in the rest of the country, but I shall not likely be believed. Nevertheless: the teachers met to try to do something about low salaries. A part-time preacher who was also a temporary principal began the discussion. He faced the group and delivered an impassioned speech on the poverty of teachers and the parsimony of lawmakers, and concluded with the suggestion that we all get in our cars and drive down to Jackson and sit on the lawn of the governor's mansion and "when he comes out beg him for a crust of bread!"

A little man jumped up suddenly in the back; he too was principal of an outlying school. "Well," he shouted, 'I know what they done in DE-troit, and I know what they done in Philadelphia! They went on strike, that's what they done!" He sat down.

Someone else spoke haltingly for a moment, and the preacher stood up down front again and said that he thought we ought to talk about this thing, but that we ought to *do* something, too. It was a serious matter, and we ought not just talk. We ought to *do* something.

The little man in the back jumped up again and shouted, "Well, I know what they done in DE-troit, and I know what they done in Philadelphia. They went on strike, that's what they done!"

A woman stood up slowly and dramatically off to the left. "I'm speaking as a mother," she said plaintively. "Now, there's people that go into the teaching profession but they aren't loyal to it, and they don't deserve any consideration. But some of us have been loyal to it all through the years, and I think it's time we had our reward.

"My husband and I are both teachers and we have stuck with it even though we could have made a lot more money doing other things. And I'm not just saying that, either, because I know we could. We took off and worked in a defense plant when they were running and made a lot more money than we ever made teaching. And I think that those who have been loyal to teaching ought to have a decent salary and some consideration."

The moderator thanked her, and said he was sure it was true, as several had said, that we all needed and deserved more money than we were getting, and he wondered if someone had a plan of action he might want to propose.

The little man in the back jumped up again, shouting, "Well, I know what they done in DE-troit, and I know what they done in Philadelphia! They went on strike, that's what they done!" He sat down.

"And did you want to put that in the form of a motion?" the moderator asked.

"Hunh?" the little man said, startled.

"Did you want to put that in the form of a motion? Are you advocating that we vote to go on strike if we don't get higher salaries?"

"No," the man said, horrified. "No, I didn't say *we* ought to go on strike. But I know what they done in DE-troit, and I know what they done in Philadelphia."

The other meeting was a large gathering of college alumni; its memorable feature appeared after a lengthy attempt from the floor to get some parliamentary order so

that we could actually function as a democratic body. The
president managed through real or assumed innocence,
however, to circumvent all reform, and just before casual
acceptance of the recommended slate of officers for the
next year, he made a classic remark: "Now fellows," he
said engagingly, blinking off yet another attack, "we're
just all here together!"

I think of a teacher who asked another to be nice and
give a particular student a passing grade in a final college
course. The boy wouldn't ever make it on his own; no
need to put him through it again for nothing. And anyway, it didn't matter. He was only going out here in the
country somewhere, and teach.

A friend of mine reported with shock a committee meeting with a high college official and the head of a department (one a minister) on financial aid to students. When
my friend happened upon the application of a particular
girl whose circumstances he knew, he immediately
showed it to the other committeemen and said, "We ought
to disqualify this one. I'm really surprised they would do
such a thing, but this report of the family income is simply a lie."

The other two men looked at him and waited a moment
and then said, "Well?"

"Well, they've falsified the application," he said.

The men shrugged. "If you had a child coming to college and wanted financial aid," one of them said, "you
would put a low figure down for income, too, wouldn't
you?"

Actually, of course, they were less disturbed by the lie
than by his calling attention to it. The whole fabric of
society was at stake.

For the safety of our way of life, one must support whatever is currently the attitude of that society, or at the least

keep his mouth shut. When a society's façade is supported by a nonexistent framework — when its education is a veneer for ignorance, its honesty for lies, its democratic processes for autocracy, its system of laws for illegality, its stability for forcible exploitation — then the least breath of dissent may blow it all down. Dissent cannot be tolerated.

When Mississippi was voting avidly for the man and his socialism, for which they now blame him but not their empty bellies of the 1930's, I was apparently the only boy in my class who came from a family opposed to Franklin D. Roosevelt. I remember well the result of a 1940 history class discussion in which I said that Wendell Willkie seemed to be a pretty good man: three or four boys took me down bodily in the basement and said that they were going to beat me up. Whether they would have if an interruption had not occurred, I do not know.

My son had somewhat the same experience at an excellent school in California, in a wealthy community, twenty years later. He quit letting people know he was for John F. Kennedy, because the kids ganged up on him. Where a given sentiment is pervasive enough, the dissenter persistent, force is, of course, the most immediate and effective weapon.

How near I came during my undergraduate days to learning that lesson at some expense to my hide, I do not know. Near enough. My error was in writing an open letter concerning campus political ethics during a heated campaign, and citing incidents and identifying people. For five nights I did not go to my rooms, because I was warned each evening that a mob of students was waiting in an alley with pipes and two-by-fours. I did not investigate the accuracy of the reports, but spent those nights with friends and family. More than once I was accosted by crowds of forty or fifty angry students, but nothing physical was done to me, although some of the students boasted openly, even in classes, that they would "get" me. There were some fights in the dormitories about the issue — the girls' dormitories — and one of my coed friends publicly castigated me in language unbecoming a Southern Belle. Some of my friends, especially a girl I had been dating and a girl I was associated with on the campus paper, were verbally attacked, as I was by the large crowds. The nearest thing to physical violence that I knowingly encountered, however, came when a small, tough athlete was sent to bring me to a gathering at which, he said, they were to beat me up. He refused to bring me, but offered to beat me up personally if I did not retract my statements in the letter. Fortunately, he was a reasonable sort, and our talk about the letter clarified its statements and its purpose to his satisfaction.

Giving the person accused or distrusted a chance to explain is quite unusual. I know intimately a situation in which a college administration accepted rumors, spread by students who had failed a course for cheating, as the basis for sanctions against the professor — without hearing him at all, because the administrators did not want to "embarrass" him by "calling him on the carpet." The same sort of thing has been reported to me from other sections of the country — with one major difference: the reason given for sanctions outside the South were the real reasons. I have never known of a firing at a Southern school for which the real reason was given. In one case I was told of, no reason was given. The teacher heard rumors that he was fired, and when he inquired, he discovered the rumors were true.

I taught at a college for a while at which a young man was removed from student office and eventually from school when he should have been commended, so far as I could judge. The incident disturbed me greatly, and I looked into it as closely as I could, although I had no authority in the matter. One evening another student brought onto the campus some students from the rival college. What started out as a lark, when the students were apprehended, turned into some mob violence, with rocks thrown at the car as the rival students were leaving, and with an accident off campus resulting in some injuries.

According to every eyewitness who would talk to me, the student who was punished was in no way responsible for what happened. On the contrary, everyone told me, he was the only person there who attempted to restore peace and who tried to protect the beleaguered boys. Two members of the student judicial council which judged him were also present at the riot (and photographed) but made no move to help. Witnesses said that one faculty member appeared and did nothing, and that the night watchman was there with his pistol on his hip, and did nothing. But a scapegoat was needed, and the only person who had acted to salvage the situation was chosen.

I mentioned all this to a colleague who, I thought, might have some access to authority; I traced through all the evidence and indicated that it seemed to me that this was an outrage, and that something must be done on the student's behalf.

"Yes," my colleague replied, "but he's always been something of a troublemaker."

XIII

Fair in Mississippi

I F I AGREE that the resentment of Mississippians toward those who come from elsewhere to correct the local situation is natural, I do not mean that it is either justified or right. Nevertheless, both Mississippians and outsiders quite naturally do resent the intrusion of moralists who point the accusing finger and say, "You're wrong."

The difference between Mississippi and much of the rest of the country is that Mississippians, in what Jim Silver rightly calls the Closed Society, resent almost equally the admission by one of her own people that "*We*'re wrong."

When I moved from Kentucky back into Mississippi in 1957 I learned of a newspaper edited in the little South Mississippi town of Petal and published principally to declare that "We're wrong." The editor, P. D. East, had written some hilarious parodies — notably a Citizens Councils ad with a braying jackass and the promise of su-

periority for only five dollars, and an editorial advocating
the crawfish as Mississippi's state symbol. One of my colleagues informed me that another had once invited East
up for dinner with a number of the more nearly liberal people around. "Excellent," I said. And since the teacher who
had feted East was now out of the state, I added, "Maybe
we could have him up again. I'd like to meet him."

The other man shook his head. "No," he said carefully.
"You wouldn't want to. He isn't, really . . . socially acceptable."

It was later, after I had been reminded over a period
of time what was and what was not socially acceptable,
that I bought a suit of clothes from a local Negro man
who took measurements and sent them off to a tailoring
company. I had known the man for years, and at his as-
surance that the suit would be a very good one and would
fit perfectly, I tried it. He was right, and for the first
time in my life I received a considerable volume of com-
pliments on my attire.

When a friend would say something nice to me about
the suit, I could seldom resist the reply, "Yeah. Bought it
from a nigger downtown." It was a remark calculated to
stop all conversation for minutes at a stretch and wreak
havoc in the depths where lurk ancient proprieties and
prejudices. The surface upheavals were fascinating.

Twice, however, silence did not ensue. One friend reacted only by inquiring into the details so that he could
order a suit himself. But another deftly turned my own
weapon back at me. My intent, insofar as it was serious,
was not to lower myself to the level that "buying a suit
from a nigger downtown" would imply in the minds of
my victims, but to raise the concept of "Negro" toward
social acceptability. This one friend, nevertheless, did not
bat an eye. "Oh, yes," he replied equably, and named the

Negro. "I've seen him going down to Farish Street with his little box of samples."

Some Mississippians, at least, were disturbed by the trend of events in those days. The White Citizens Councils were getting underway, and before long the state itself would be giving money to that organization for the purpose of guaranteeing the supremacy of half its citizens over the other half. I have never seen a Citizens Councils charter or constitution, or whatever they have, but an older friend of mine told me that it was easy enough to organize a chapter. All you had to do was get five men together and agree to support a list of aims. He said that the aims as stated were not bad — it was the understood application of them that was bad. He suggested that we get three other local men of like mind with us and, before a rumored segregationist chapter formed in the town, organize the only Citizens Councils chapter in the state actually to live up to its professed ideals.

I thought it was an excellent idea, although it was dangerous. My friend had a great deal to lose, but he was willing to risk it; and so we began trying to list the men in the town who might possibly go along with us — and we were able to come up with only four names, including our own.

There were other attempts at enlightenment we could make, however. For the five most recent years that I taught in Mississippi and Louisiana colleges, there was not a single class I can recall in which the race question did not come up at some time during the semester. It has seemed evident to me that if one is to teach students to read and to write, one has to see to it that they think, at least slightly, and thinking cannot occur in a pre-set mind with built-in checks against all deviation and doubt. So, for instance, I have had to show basic deistic concepts to be apparently irrefutable, given certain generally accepted premises and a standard pattern of logic, so that Southern Baptist students will not dismiss Alexander Pope as simply stupid for not writing exactly the same thing they read in their local church bulletins. However wrong, not stupid. Not many students are so literally bound, of course, but all are to a degree. Some are worse. Some can read through the *Essay on Man,* or Emerson's "Self-Reliance," or Henley's "I am the captain of my fate," or Bryant's "Thanatopsis," and come out with an orthodox Baptist sermon as a paraphrase. They get it from their elders.

The process is the same, of course, wherever there is any sort of orthodoxy, and is nowhere more evident than in those communities which by inculcation believe in many of the particulars I am even now sympathizing with. But my work was in the South, and it was my job to try, not to impose my thought upon the students, but to open their minds to the possibility of thought. And I believe, too, that a teacher needs, often, to let his own stand be known so that the student can with less confusion judge the bias of the lectures. So it was that in every class I allowed discussion of the racial issues, tried to see to it that no assumptions on any side went unchallenged and unexamined, and tried to make clear that no one was to take my point of view because I was an "authority," that each person was responsible for his own relationship with fact and with truth, but that I believed the policy of the state of Mississippi was basically unconstitutional, undemocratic, immoral, un-Christian, and humanly reprehensible, though many of the people who supported its policy had no such intentions. That, further, we should abolish segregation even if we were not forced to, because it was, simply put, wrong. The discussion would be heated, often, but free.

I thought, then, that my position was reasonably clear. One day, however, the question came up again; discussion raged for a while; and somebody asked me, finally, in some exasperation, "Well, what do *you* believe?" I tried to state my belief succinctly. When I was well into it I noticed the reaction of one of the students; he was reasonably competent, good solid average in grades and capable of better. Since he was taking his third course with me, it seemed strange that his face should turn pale and then gradually flush scarlet. It took him a few minutes to get his voice and demand of me in horrified disbelief, "You mean you're an integrationist?"

In vain, son. In vain.

The Citizens Councils had a female spy on the campus (unless she was lying) who also read books for them to determine which were subversive, and who reported that three faculty members were on the Citizens Councils "list," presumably the same list which eventually included some eighty organizations, such as the Episcopal Church and, as I recall it, the United States Air Force. But none of us there suffered in any obvious way for our point of view. I have never known whether I made the list, even; there must at one time have been eight or ten faculty members who were at least in private against segregation. Briefly at one time perhaps four or five were more or less openly so.

But other people were not so fortunately undisturbed in their efforts to do something about the situation in Mississippi, even though some of them were, I understand, segregationists. Hazel Brannon Smith, editor of the Lexington *Advertiser* and Durant *News,* began to have difficulties, as the editor of a rival newspaper told me.

He said that Hazel's picture, unknown to her, had been printed in *Ebony.* The text cited her for trying to be simply fair, regardless of race. However, the magazine

was discovered by a Citizens Councils member who held
it up at a meeting without any reading of the text. It and
she were denounced. I was told that then pressures began
to be applied; that her husband was removed from his
job; that a rival newspaper and printing shop was being
set up and subsidized, and that merchants were being
warned against advertising in her papers or placing printing orders with her. A school at which a junior college
journalism convention met had been "forced" to withdraw
an invitation for her to speak.

That has been nowhere near the end of economic and
physical harassment, of course; but Hazel still has a following in Mississippi (I was told of her getting a tremendous reception when she spoke at a meeting early in 1964,
for instance), and she was awarded a Pulitzer Prize in
1964 for her editorials: not a happy ending, but a better
midpoint than could be confidently expected. After all,
she had been fair, and that is a crime against injustice.

Being fair in Mississippi is, I believe, a bigger task than
anyone outside can imagine. Although certain principles
are clear — when viewed in perspective, at any rate —
they do not exist in the abstract, and being on the "right"
side does not automatically make a man right.

In the summer of 1961 I received, in California, a letter
from a friend in Mississippi who had concerned himself
with what was going on and so witnessed firsthand many
of the Freedom Rider incidents. He wrote, in part:

> . . . I think it fair and objective to say . . . that a good
> many reports from Jackson — a chief offender being the
> Examiner of San Francisco — are not only inaccurate and
> unbalanced, but sometimes false.
>
> I am thinking of the Examiner stories I have read, and
> I know, for I was standing there when the reporter in-

quired, that (Examiner, June 22, by John Bryan): "Asked why the sentence has been upped from a $200 fine to two months in jail and a $200 fine and then the present maximum under Mississippi law, the judge just smiled" . . . His report is a lie, since Spencer answered: "We announced some time ago this indulgence — this leniency — would stop if the Riders kept coming." Judge Spencer didn't even smile (he very seldom does).

In the same story Bryan reports that a Capt. Ralph Hargrove was the only witness at the trial. Fact is, Capt. J. L. Ray is the testifying (and arresting) officer, and [Hargrove] is photographer and records man. This could be a natural mistake, of course, mistaking names.

But he records the trial proceedings (always putting "trial" in quotes), noting the goodnaturedness of the trial and more especially the brevity (five minutes). He does *not* say that the trial he is covering is the tenth or twelfth such in the past couple of weeks, and they are really getting Old Hat by now. There *is* goodnaturedness on the part of the judge and both attorneys, with the witness, who is always Capt. Ray. Defense Attorney Jack Young now says (his only question): "Capt. Ray, if I asked you substantially the same questions now as I have asked you in previous cases of this nature, would your answers be substantially the same?" Capt. Ray says, "Yes, they would." Young then says, "No further questions."

Bryan also says that at the suggestion of Chief of Detectives M. B. Pierce he "talked to local Negroes." But he says he talked to — and quotes at length — Richard Haley, whom he identifies as local field secretary for CORE. Haley — whom I know . . . — came here a few days after the first Rider wave. He is CORE field secretary in Chicago.

There are quite a few other examples.

I must also say in fairness that I have seen the Riders in their cells a number of times, and have been through

the maximum security unit at Parchman, and a goodly
number of "smuggled reports" on conditions are not true
. . . while not air conditioned, the jails are comfortable,
as jails go . . .

Now, you know me to be as concerned about civil
rights as any Rider. But frankly I get frustrated sometimes when you see such violations of fairness on both
sides. I am not in sympathy with the city or the state,
and even if I were I think I would recognize that with
the present federal situation and on the basis of precedents
to this, any adversity to such demands is futile and only
accomplishes a stalling for time.

But I get disturbed — equally, I suppose — at extremists
on either side. I wish somebody would just start telling
the truth, dammit . . .

You see, I am in a funny position, and am sort of confused at things. Not confused about what to believe, but
at why people choose to lie to themselves and/or others.

Why can't people who seem otherwise intelligent
enough look at things and be honest about it? It's a little
disturbing. Why should such people as the Riders, who
have a good case, choose to lie or embellish their stories?
(Cases in point: "smuggled letters" from Riders telling
how they are forced to pick cotton on the county farm
in 97 degree heat, when there is no cotton on the county
farm, when it's not cotton picking time anyway, and when
the temperature has not been even to 90; false stories of
brutality or unbearable conditions.) I think it's a false
society that lies about itself — equality of opportunity,
voter registration, etc. Then I find assault on that false
society by another kind of falsity. And if you're concerned
about the principle of truth, then both are flatly and
equally wrong.

I'm sure the concern is not new or unique, but in this
place and to me it is puzzling . . .

XIV

For Very Shame

THE DILEMMA of the liberal or moderate or individualist in Mississippi has been a very real one. Often he has had to decide when, where, and how loudly to speak out, knowing that just one shout can bring on, in effect, laryngitis — no one will hear anything else he says. And the original shout will be heeded little if at all.

My sister is a missionary to Nigeria, sent by the Southern Baptist Foreign Mission Board. The Oxford riot convinced her that she should make her appeal directly to the Baptists back home; she sent a letter to the *Mississippi Baptist Record*. It was printed on November 15, 1962:

Dear Friends,

What do you expect of us? You send us out here to preach that Christ died for all men. Then you make a travesty of our message by refusing to associate with some of them just because of the color of their skin.

You have entrusted to us the words of Life, to proclaim for you to the people of Nigeria that in Christ all men are equal. You are supposed to be holding the lifelines for us, and you are twisting them into a noose of racism to strangle our message. You send us out here to proclaim the Good News, and then cut the ground from under our feet.

Some time ago one of the most prominent leaders of the Nigerian Baptist Convention told this poignant story. He was in the States studying for a theological degree. One day he bathed very carefully, as is his habit, dressed in nice clean clothes, and put on freshly polished shoes, tied his tie very carefully and went out to eat. At the restaurant he was sold food, but was told to take it outside to eat it. He smiled, with his lips, and did so. Now, what could this man have done to be acceptable to the white man behind the restaurant counter? He is a man of God; the Holy Spirit dwells in him; he is an upright man, a man of impeccable character; he was absolutely clean, dressed in acceptable clothes, using acceptable manners; but he is black. What can he do about that? Why should he feel that he has to do anything about being black? What kind of hideousness have we allowed to take charge of our hearts and minds that makes it utterly impossible for a fellow human being to be acceptable to us just because he is the color God made him?

Deep down inside, where the Holy Spirit dwells, many of you feel about this the way I do. Why are you just sitting there doing nothing about it? You know very well that if there had been a color bar in Paul's day, he would have said in Galatians 3:28, "There is neither Jew nor Greek, there is neither bond nor free, there is neither male nor female, there is neither black nor white for ye are all one in Christ Jesus," since he was calling attention to the fact that Christ has wiped out all distinctions, social or otherwise, from between those who follow Him. Oh, if we could only say, "But the Christians do not have this sort of prejudice." What a testimony that would be!

When you know what the will of the Lord is, why are you silent? Are you afraid your business will be hurt? Jesus says, "Your father knows you have need of all these things, but seek ye first the kingdom of God and His righteousness." Are you afraid of hurting those who are near and dear to you? So you may, so you may. Ross Barnett is my cousin, and in writing this letter, I am wounding some of the dearest people in the world, but Jesus says, "He that loves father or mother more than Me is not worthy of Me."

You are closing the door of Africa in our faces. The Communists do not need to work against the preaching of the gospel here by Americans; you are doing it quite adequately. Wake up! Look at what is happening in the world! Be Courageous; act like *Christians!*

ANTONINA CANZONERI

There was some response. I was told that one direct result was a resolution favorable to her position drawn up at the Mississippi Baptist Convention, that the resolution was watered down and watered down and finally tabled. Some people spoke to family members, privately, to say that she was right and they were glad she had spoken out. She received a few letters thanking her for her stand. Ira Harkey of the Pascagoula *Chronicle,* already under (literal) fire, ran a favorable editorial, and so did Hazel Brannon Smith. The following are excerpts from Mary Cain's *The Summit Sun;* Mrs. Cain quotes Hazel before attacking Antonina:

FOR VERY SHAME, MISS CANZONERI!

"In view of the timidity of state Baptists to express Christian conviction of racial good will in resolutions offered at

the annual convention last week, we imagine the Canzoneri letter will arouse conflicting emotions," wrote Hazel
Brannon Smith in her four newspapers last week. "But it
should be read by all those who profess Christianity, all
those who are interested in the image America tries to
present to the world as a democratic freedom-loving,
Christian nation which respects the dignity and rights of
all men." She then quoted in its entirety a letter which
appeared in a recent issue of the Baptist Record written
by Baptist missionary Antonina Canzoneri, who is in
Nigeria, West Africa. Her barbs were directed to Mississippi in particular and, indirectly, at Gov. Ross Barnett,
who is said to be her cousin.

Miss Canzoneri has added nothing new to the same old
cry of the integrationists and we consider the publication
of her letter a waste of precious space. She apparently
has no knowledge of her Baptist heritage or she would not
be crying out for all the world to fit her pattern for living.
Freedom of conscience is a basic Baptist tenet and when
it ceases to be so, we relinquish our membership in this
great denomination.

The "racial good will" is there, among Christians of all
races, creeds and colors, and needs no pointing up, except
for the fact that RACES is the key word: separate as the
fingers on one's hand, never losing racial identity, but one
as children of God, black or white.

Not long ago our church was visited by a missionary who
held views similar to those of Miss Canzoneri. We argued,
albeit fruitlessly, with him, as we would with her, that it
is not the Christians who are letting the missions down,
but on the contrary, it is the missionaries who violate their
sacred trust when they do not emphasize to the people
whom they seek to win to Christ, the importance of racial
integrity and the service the South has rendered the nation
in its determination to maintain it.

Mrs. Cain quotes Albert Schweitzer against fraternization, laments Antonina's having listened to propaganda, concedes her right to live among Negroes, and continues:

> ... but she should be ashamed to talk down to the Christian people who made it possible for her to take Christ's message of salvation to the lost people of Nigeria. We venture to hope that she understands the plan of salvation better than she does the foundations of her denomination.

And perhaps, after all, she has rendered Southern Baptists a service by pinpointing an issue that apparently needs clarification: Shall Southern Baptist people continue to strip themselves of necessities to keep in the field missionaries who do not expound the basic Baptist creed of freedom of conscience, led of God?

"Start acting like Christians," Miss Canzoneri? — For very shame!

(One good Baptist remarked, "I haven't seen any Southern Baptists stripping themselves of the necessities to keep missionaries in the field, have you?")

Antonina also got a number of unfavorable letters, mostly from members of the Women's Missionary Union. Some threatened to withhold missionary money, others said they would give in spite of her. Virtually all spoke of racial separation as ordained by God, and some brought in the redbirds and bluebirds. President Kennedy, the NAACP and the Communists were generally considered one body devoted to the destruction of Mississippi and God's way of life. A few direct quotations:

> I did not know that our foreign missionaries were sent to encourage their converts to come to this country and *live* with us. I thought you were sent to *tell* them of Christ to save their souls, and to teach them, and help *them,* to *help themselves.*

And certainly God does not intend for us . . . to mix the races (I am speaking of marrying and intermarrying and not just associate and mingle with them because we do that and thought nothing of it until the stupid ignorant leaders have tried to force integration down our throats which only leads to mixing the races).

I too am a Southern Baptist and I know that all men are created of God and precious in His sight. I don't have a thing against anyone — white, yellow, red, or black. I love every one, and I wouldn't mistreat any one deliberately.

Our missionary Society gives money every year to the Lottie Moon Christmas offering, and we know a portion of it goes to work with Negroes in Africa and other places.

In your letter you told about the Nigerian who went into the white restaurant to be served and the man refused to let him eat with the white people. If he had made allowances for that one, he would have had to make them for others. If the man didn't want to serve a Negro in his restaurant, I think that comes under the category of his business. Do you eat and sleep with them? The man in the restaurant couldn't look in the Nigerian's heart and see how good a Christian he was. I'm sure the Nigerian didn't think nearly as much about it as you did. Christians are willing to suffer hardships, embarrassments, and other things for Christ's sake.

And one letter, having blasted John Kennedy, "Stupid Brother," his "wealth and Catholic Fathers," etc., concludes with, "If I am wrong in my belief I pray that God will forgive me."

Not "show me the light," but "forgive me." And this basic reluctance goes to great depths. A ministerial student argued intensely with me on the race question until, thinking to shift the argument, I said, "Suppose you discovered tomorrow that you were half Negro."

"I couldn't. I know better than *that*."

"Well, say an eighth. A sixteenth. That would be enough. There would be some changes, wouldn't there?"

He was silent a moment and then he assented briefly.

"You'd change your mind about some of these things, wouldn't you?"

He shook his head. "No. Not that." The look on his face was very strange. I thought I knew what he had in mind.

"You'd shoot yourself?"

He nodded, apparently quite serious.

"Ah, come on," I said. "You think the Negro really is in a terrible situation, then."

"Look," he said, "I've been this way twenty-three years and I couldn't make that change now."

How does one work to change the mind that wants forgiveness but never correction, the mind that must retain its own concept of itself and the world or be destroyed? And of course that sort of mind has become a principal feature of the Deep South.

Another ministerial student had been pastor of a Southern church for several years. He and his family were well liked and believed that the church members were their very good friends as well as fellow Christians. The young man became concerned with the habitual ministerial silence on the Christian approach to the Negro, and he worked on a sermon dealing with the subject. When he preached by invitation at a neighboring church, he tried the sermon there first. People listened attentively and were very nice to him afterwards.

He either forgot or never knew that politeness to a "stranger" who will not be back next Sunday is quite other than genuine acceptance or even tolerance, and so he preached the sermon with some confidence at his home church. Within three days he was fired and moved out. And that was that.

He was not alone. Twenty-eight Methodist ministers once lost their churches in Mississippi for a stand on the race issue. But perhaps the most convincing and moving case of all was that of a Jackson minister known for years as the best preacher around and as an excellent pastor. He had served nearly twenty years at the Jackson church when he discovered one Sunday that the ushers had turned Negroes away at the door.

According to the apparently true account, he told his church that if in all these years he had taught them no more of the principle of love than that, he must be a failure, and so he was offering his resignation. The church accepted it readily.

XV

The Least Misuse of Wind

IN SPITE OF all evidence, I don't think I viscerally believed the Civil War until the Oxford riot in 1962, when
mobs of students and outsiders stormed the Lyceum Building at Ole Miss while federal marshals held them off with
tear gas, and a French newsman and a local man were
killed mysteriously at the fringes of the riot. I believed
that James Meredith should be admitted to Ole Miss and
must be admitted; I believed then and I believe now that
the stand the state took was a criminal and murderous defense of an erroneous doctrine designed to protect its own
despotism. If I had had to fight, it would have been
against Mississippi; if we all had had to choose, many of
my friends and family would have fought with Mississippi.
Suddenly, in the midst of violence on ground I knew well
— violence heard through a sequence of small radio voices,
excited and often confused — I knew that the Civil War
had really taken place.

I had followed the preliminaries to the riot as well as I could from Louisiana, and the day of the riot built and built toward violence in a stream of vacillations and stupidities which angered and frightened me. Then there was the riot itself. And then word of the death of the newsman. Few things have ever affected me the way that did. I had watched the course of Mississippi lead wrongheadedly, stubbornly, to that night; I had seen the craft of the politicians, with that particular soothing voice saying that everything was going to work out all right, and with that particular gleam of the eye as some new subterfuge was expounded, and I had been amazed over and over again at how decent folk could watch and listen and not at all see where the state leaders were inevitably leading.

You couldn't tell anybody. You could predict, but nobody would listen. Not even if you went back and showed, after the fact, that you had predicted correctly, and had predicted not by means of stars and signs or by intuition, but by watching the course of events with your eyes open and in focus, by not averting your eyes. I spent an afternoon arguing to a cousin of mine, before his 1961 speeches for segregation in California, that not only was segregation wrong, it was an invitation to disaster. He insisted it was the only way to keep order in our time. In less than two years the riot occurred.

In 1963 I spoke to a poetry class at Ole Miss and attempted to respond to questions about some of my own poems that had been distributed in advance. One poem, "Sandstorm," had appeared in the *Saturday Review* that January, but had been written in California in 1961. The class had argued with their professor about the meaning of the final lines, particularly, and so they asked me what I had had in mind. The lines ran:

> The least misuse
> Of wind is hell where everything is loose.

I went back into the poem to show that it was not only an account of a real sandstorm, but that the imagery throughout was designed to apply to Mississippi's situation, and that the ending was a rather obvious reference to wind as used by a demagogue. Several students looked quite disappointed, perhaps unbelieving, and so I said further that it had taken no great insight for anyone looking on and knowing anything about Mississippi to see that some such thing as the Oxford riot was in the offing. I discovered after the class that the professor had said virtually the same thing about the poem. Both of us, I'm afraid, to no good purpose.

Mississippians, having been told over and over by their exploiters that all outside news sources consistently lie and are Communist-controlled, and having found a few actual examples of false news reports, forget the lies in their own newspapers and forget that rumor is never reliable. After the riot there were stories, believed by intelligent people, of coeds killed and children beaten by the federal marshals. These stories were circulated by politicians and newspapers as well as by word of mouth among the citizens. Not a single corpse has ever shown up, nobody has ever been able to locate the beaten children, and no white people have mysteriously disappeared. Obviously, the stories were lies, intentional or not. But the same people who believed that "outside" newsmen were lying still believe exactly that. The same people who believed that the local news sources and the politicans and the Citizens Councils were telling the truth still so believe. In every case that I have been able to check about which the majority of national news sources disagreed with the standard local story, the local story has turned out to be demonstrably wrong — yet that fact has not shaken Mississippi's belief in the local version of whatever comes up next.

One Mississippian told me at the time, "Just wait till Senator Eastland's committee gets through investigating this thing, and you'll see." I replied that in spite of his vow at the time, Senator Eastland would never investigate, because he knew that what he found would be totally unpalatable to the state. The fact that the Senator somehow never did get around to investigating has not apparently shaken that person's belief that if he had done as he promised, it would have shown that the marshals were wrong. However, the eyewitness account of Jim Silver, for instance, published in letters to the editor and now in his book, *Mississippi: The Closed Society,* is not even to be read. Far too many Mississippians so prejudge.

My point is that those who wonder why Mississippi hasn't been shown the error of its ways need to memorize the maxim an excellent former teacher of mine promulgated in a committee meeting. "Well," she said, "don't expect any intelligence to be used." The warning is universally applicable.

In California recently I argued politics with a bright young man for an evening. He lamented the fact, first, that people vote on the basis of personality rather than on the issues. We began arguing the issues, and he eventually agreed with me on each one as we went down the line. Finally he was left with no stated support for any portion of his candidate's platform. "Well?" I said, a bit triumphantly.

He shook his head briefly. "Well, I still think I'll vote for him. I just somehow don't *like* his opponent."

Part of my own reaction to the Oxford incident was

right out of the Mississippi mind I have been trying to identify. After the riot was over, the thing that impressed me most was that the coeds on the Ole Miss campus were not Polite; they did not act like young ladies. They literally stood around James Meredith and shouted "Nigger!" like common Northern slum-bred viragos, and although my response to the riot had been anger and grief and outrage, my response to such behavior by Mississippi college girls was shock and near disbelief. I wanted by some means to discredit the television pictures, because I knew better. Those nice girls just wouldn't act that way.

Of course, national news coverage reaches into the Deep South, but it can be turned off either at the set or at the mind. The morning after the riot, a student asked me with what I thought was a Rebel sneer to comment on the riot. I did so at some length, and, still caught up in the intensity of my feelings, I turned to the student and demanded, "So now, what have you got to say?"

He held up his hand and said, "Slow down! I really think I've learned something, but I can only take in so much at a time. I don't know what I think." After class two or three students told me that they had never known there was "another side." Of course, they had heard another side — that is, it had come at them through the national news media, but it had penetrated not at all. Again and again in the next weeks I was to hear that same response: "I have never heard this side of the thing at all."

Some people in Mississippi began to speak out, some of the Ole Miss faculty, a few ministers, some businessmen (most to recant soon); there were the favorable responses to my sister's letter. But the mood of the state seemed not to change for the better. Then the following summer Medgar Evers was assassinated in Jackson, and again a few spoke out. The most eloquent comment I know of ap-

peared in the June 22, 1963, *Clarion-Ledger,* a letter to
the editor written by my good friend Evans Harrington,
a professor at Ole Miss:

Dear Editor:
   Mississippians from the governor down have expressed
shock, shame, and dismay at the murder of Medgar Evers,
and certainly I share these emotions. But in the interest
of the psychic well-being of the state I feel that a word
of caution is in order. Medgar Evers is, of course, by no
means the first Negro to be murdered in our state, even
within recent years. Nor, barring something approaching
a miracle, will he be even close to the last.
   Let us face it clearly: Our way of life is based on keeping the Negro downtrodden — under-paid, unrepresented
in government, and excluded from our own society. Now
only an ignorant or a supine and powerless people will
allow themselves to be so downtrodden. And, manifestly,
Negroes in our state are no longer any of these things.
Leaders like Medgar Evers are informing them, bolstering
their courage and initiative, and welding them into a
powerful force. Naturally, therefore, it will continue to be
necessary to kill Negro leaders; and, as the people themselves become more enlightened, it will be necessary to
kill many of them, more and more as time goes on.
   This is where the psychic damage to our state appears.
If we are to feel shock, shame, and dismay every time our
way of life brings on an assassination, every time our politicians and newspapermen and other spokesmen trade on
and inflame ignorance and race hatred to the point of murder, will we not eventually be overwhelmed with shock,
shame, and dismay? Will we not finally be forced to take
the logical last step in the long series of withdrawal symp-
toms which we have already manifested? How much
shock, shame, and dismay can a people endure without
turning their state into a psychiatric ward?

The solution to this problem is obvious. If we are to continue in our present objectives, we must accept murder as an integral, even a normal, part of our way of life. We must school ourselves not to feel genuine shock or shame at the assassination of our opponents. Naturally, we should continue to profess shock and shame, at least as long as we are forced by economic and military deficiencies to maintain relationships with democratic countries like the United States. But privately we should learn from other strong and successful peoples who have championed racial superiority and state sovereignty. Consider, for instance, how far Hitler and his Nazis would have gotten in building their master race and state supremacy if they had felt shock, shame, and dismay at the murdering of Jews and other enemies.

There may, however, be a few among us not quite ready to slough off the decadent democratic timidity concerning murder. There may be some with quaint consciences who cannot escape shock, shame, and even a modicum of grief at the mindless slaughter of good, brave men. To these recidivists I offer this last desperate consolation: Mississippi, after all, did produce Medgar Evers, a man who (oh rare!) would not learn to be "practical" or "shrewd," would not learn to serve whimsical Time and brutal Circumstance, would not accept a definition of his "place" laid down by someone else (the kind of someone who would skulk in a thicket and shoot him in the back for disagreeing). Here was a man who knew precisely how much he was risking and why, and who had the courage and ultimate intelligence to do so; and I, witnessing his conduct, even from the distance of newspaper stories and television programs, have felt myself grow a dimension in aspiration and resolution, an emotion I have not experienced in watching many white Mississippians in recent times.

Even more hopefully, Evers was not unique in these

respects among his people in our state. Mississippi has a number of Negroes (concern for THEIR lives forbids naming them) whose courage, intelligence, and integrity fill many with awe and inspiration. As long as we continue to produce our Everses, even to be murdered by our way of life, we are not completely hopeless. And maybe, in some unforeseeable future, they will even teach us their courage and idealism.

It was about this time that I received a letter from a former student. She had been involved in a discussion of the race issue in a class during the previous year, and when the religious aspect had arisen, I had said that I defied anybody to defend his segregationism on the basis of two basic commandments of Jesus, two which served most obviously as the description of the Christian way of life: Do unto others as you would have them do unto you, and Love thy neighbor as thyself. Tears welled up in the girl's eyes. That was all I knew by way of background, but that picture was quite vivid in my mind.

She wrote, in part:

> Two other students and I used to hold spirited conversations about the subject of racial prejudice. Naturally, what you said about the subject influenced our opinions a great deal. I might add that this influence was for the better. Thanks to you we are all rabid integrationists now. When I came home and told my family about my change of heart I really gave them a shock. My . . . brother now has serious doubts about my sanity.

Perhaps others can read this letter with equanimity, but it hurts me. It pleases me, too, however, and some other students' reactions merely depress. You see the light of reason dawning in their eyes, and soon there is an intelligent and even bold comment, and one day they come up after class and discuss things with growing interest; you begin to see them come alive and walk with a new sort of purpose. And then the semester ends; at registration they stop to speak a moment; a couple of weeks later they wave across campus; and after a month when you meet them in the hallway they avoid your eyes.

To the girl who wrote the letter you want to say, "Now, don't go so far with this that it disrupts your family and makes you unhappy." And then you pass the averted face in the hallway and you know better.

Not long ago a friend of mine did some teaching in his home state in the South, working with Negroes in remedial classes. He wrote:

A few weeks ago, when I was home, a few of the assistants here (including one Negro) decided to go for a ride, wound up in [my home town], and naturally called. I couldn't go anywhere with them, but did ride out to the filling station they called from. Meanwhile, they had been refused use of the restroom; I pulled up about the same time the police did. Nothing happened (nothing was even said), but I was seen talking to an integrated group. Tho I wasn't recognized, it only took a day or so for my license number to be checked through [the state capital] and for the rumors to build up to respectable proportions. This info got back to town about the same time that the Negro porter in our store decided to integrate a local cafe. Naturally he was seen as an "agent" of [the family business], and these two "incidents" were a little strong for a town like ——. My uncle who runs the store had a hard time for a while (people threatening to close accounts unless the boy were fired, etc.). Not being one to jeopardize economic or social acceptance for such trifles as morality or law, he did fire him (but in a sly manner —

thus avoiding conflict with the new Civil Rights Act). It is the utmost irony that some of the wilder rumors had him as local representative of the NAACP!

Of course the maverick who speaks out, or the dissenter who is brought out into the open as not-a-good-Southerner in the currently accepted Southern definition of the term, is thought of by his family as a traitor to all we have always held dear, but that very quirk of memory puzzles many of us. An old friend of mine was away from the South for a couple of years, not long ago, at the same time I was away for a time. We both visited our homes in Mississippi, and then later discussed from outside the state what we had encountered.

"It wasn't that way before," he said. "They have all changed. And now we can't go back because of the very morals they taught us when we were growing up."

XVI

On the Front Porch

I f THE DILEMMA of the "enlightened" Southerner is a real one and a difficult one, what of the situation of the Negro, who not only is by definition not a Southerner but has none of the white man's considerable immunity to oppression? It's really hard to say, from the outside. It is obvious that "learning to think" is even more dangerous for the Negro and that any sort of education is likely to lead, economically, not much of anywhere.

When I commented on the efficiency and intelligence of our garbage man in Louisiana, I was told that he is actually highly educated. He owns and runs the business, I understand, and possibly makes good money, but an ignorant white bank clerk has at least more pleasant working conditions. A cultivated Negro waitress there turned out to have two years of college. A janitor had some college training.

Unquestionably, then, the Negro has had all too little to gain by education, even when he could get it. And attempts to gain status as white people gain status have been met with extreme measures — when one Mississippi Negro farmer painted his house, nightriders attacked it with fire and gunshots. According to reports, he was arrested for resisting. For a Negro to respond to a white man the way another white man would has long been punishable by verbal and physical abuse and by economic retaliation. In short, the Negro has had greater reason to remain quietly and in relative safety within the narrow bounds of his "contented" culture than have even Southern whites. But the younger generation has come up less than the younger Southern whites in conservative imitation of their elders.

Some time ago I was taken by a white friend to visit two Negro brothers. There was quite some difference in the ages of the two, and even more in background. The younger brother had decided as a boy that he wanted to see the country, and so he had worked his way over much of the United States. Later he had been in the Army, and now he was working on a farm. He was never discourteous or presumptuous, but he stood squarely on his own two feet and spoke with neither fear nor apology, and with obvious intelligence. He was ready and able to accept me as his equal and to accept the fact that he was mine — and, often a more difficult proposition, to accept my acceptance. If the language is confusing, the situation is more so; but once the series of acceptances is made, and if no outside forces intervene, whatever problems remain are merely personal.

The older brother had lived in rural Mississippi all his life. It was to his home we went. Whether it belonged to him or he worked the land for someone else, I do not know, and I did not see the place by daylight. We drove out gravel roads for some distance and turned off onto a dirt drive. I opened a gate and closed it after the car, and then we pulled on down in front of a very small house, visible dimly in the moonlight. We walked through another gate into the yard, mostly bare dirt, and up two or three wooden steps to the porch. Thin posts supported the roof. The porch was narrow and ran along the entire front of the house. There were two front doors. Sitting in straight chairs on the porch, four of us took up virtually half the porch; the rest of the family had to use the other door to go out and in.

My friend introduced me to the older brother, who nodded profusely and shook my proffered hand. "Sit down. Sit down," he said. Then he sat gingerly in his own chair and said, "It's just a honor to have white folks come visit us."

Awkwardly, I'm afraid, I tried to tell him that that was not at all the way we felt about it, that we were aware that whiteness of skin did not make people better than other people, and that actually my own concern was with the fact that too many white people thought otherwise and were determined to abuse black people for that reason. He did not launch into any enthusiastic agreement, and I have often wondered in such cases how surely the practiced Negro might be able to look into us and know that in spite of all our good intentions he must withhold some part of himself or he will trigger off, somewhere down the line, a set response that we are not aware of, but that will hurt all the worse for the ease and good fellowship by which it is reached.

He did talk. We sat on the small porch and looked out

at the moonlight on the dust and the nearby trees, and on the mule wandering by the yard fence, and we talked. They served watermelon. The older brother's wife came out and sat in a straight chair on the ground at the end of the porch, just out of my sight. She would not sit on the porch with us; perhaps because there was too little room or perhaps because that was the men's place, I don't know.

We talked about all kinds of things, from dipping snuff to eating hot peppers to the stupidity of some white people she had once worked for. Though that last was aimed at particular people, whose follies were cited for laughter as well as contempt, and not at white people in general, still it was the nearest thing we heard to a critical approach to the racial situation. There was a kind of general and vague agreement with us white people that the situation needed improvement, but no antagonism was expressed, and really no specific problems were considered.

One brief scene sticks in my mind: the older man with his hat off (not, apparently, in deference — just the way he happened to be handling it at the moment) and held over his heart quite motionlessly as he listened to his wife tell a favorite story. He sat facing me, not three feet away, with his dark face quite visible in the moonlight and some light from the doorway, his graying hair thin around his forehead, his features immobile, waiting, and his eyes absolutely alight.

I could not see his wife, sitting beyond and below him, but she began her story about a cousin of hers who loved hot peppers and was visiting them many years before, and how she loved hot peppers too, and how her husband really couldn't eat them. She was interrupted a couple of times by a remark on the porch or by a problem of one of the children and each time she merely stopped talking at whatever point the interruption came and resumed talking as soon as it ended, with no hint that any lapse had occurred. And all the time her husband sat, waiting for the punchline, with his hat over his heart.

She told about cooking some turnip greens, and how her cousin chopped up a whole hot pepper on his plate, and then she chopped up one on her plate, and her husband, not to be outdone, chopped up one on his plate. They began to eat, and in a moment her husband, she said, looked up and declared, "Anybody say that ain't hot is a goddam fool."

She said, "I looked at him real sharp and said, 'Are you calling me a goddam fool?'

"And he said, 'Naw, I ain't calling you nothing. But anybody say that ain't hot is a goddam fool.' "

Here her husband broke into the laughter he had been waiting for all that time, and she joined in. It was, as she told it, hilarious, and more than that it was a glimpse into a relationship that seemed, there in the moonlight and still night air, easy and comfortable and pleasant.

The younger brother said little while we were there, but I talked with him further as he drove us back. He told me about his adventures in traveling over the country as a boy, and about how he had been stopped in many places by the police. He said that some people resented being stopped and questioned, but he didn't. When you're a stranger, he said, you don't know but what somebody has just robbed a store, or something, and the police have to stop you and find out about you, since they don't know you. He said that he always cooperated, feeling sure that since he had done nothing, they would do nothing to him. And they had always let him go, except in Mississippi, he said. There he had been jailed a couple of times — for bootlegging, I believe.

Then he added that he had worked as a truck driver, among other things, and that, not just in the South, but in every part of the country there were places where you could arrive after hours and hours of steady driving and be unable to find any place to eat or sleep. No place at all.

The older brother stayed at home and had a place to eat and sleep: a shack, sustained by a wife and family, a sense of humor, and the necessity to think it an honor to have white folks visit him. The younger brother had found no place outside the state, outside his home, and had returned to the location, though never to the attitude. And anybody say that ain't hot is a goddam fool.

XVII

Among Themselves

COMPARED TO WHAT it used to be, the lot of the Negro and white Mississippians is visibly improved, if the economic aspect of living is the only consideration. Every driveway, whether concrete or dirt, sports a car or two; television aerials sprout from even the most ramshackle of houses. Seldom, outside the very poorest rural areas, do you see a large number of people in their workaday overalls when they go to town on Saturday.

The white housing developments spreading rapidly around most cities and towns are filled with attractive homes; boats on trailers are common either in or beside the carport. There is an air of prosperity that we could not have imagined back in the thirties. No question, Mississippi has come a long way economically.

Yet there are still areas in which the conditions of the poorer folk are much like those of the depression, and it is often federal supports that allow the white farmer to send his children and cars to the state universities and join them to fraternities and sororities. The Negro sections of the cities are still so depressed that the majority of white people cannot conceive of living on so low a level.

Essentially, although there is some deviation, white society runs from upper middle class downward through lower middle class, to poor. Negro society runs from lower middle class down and down.

Aside from other factors, the state, controlled by a passion for its status quo, has fostered a tightly knit centralization of economic and political interests, so that it is an easy matter to set arbitrary rates for such things as public utilities and insurance.

When we moved back to Mississippi from the Blue Grass section of Kentucky in 1957, I thought that on the same salary I would have had in Kentucky I could live somewhat better in Mississippi, since the economy was generally lower there. I was wrong. First there was the 4 percent sales and use tax on nearly everything, including food. At that time Kentucky had no sales tax, though one was inaugurated soon afterward. State income taxes in Kentucky did not reach down to my level, but I was liable to a small income tax in Mississippi. Later Ross Barnett would have income taxes lowered — on the upper levels. My telephone bill went up 50 percent for the same service in the same sort of situation. Food prices were fully as high as in Kentucky, if not higher, except for bananas. It cost as much to heat our Mississippi house in the milder winters with cheap natural gas as it had cost with coal in the snows of Kentucky. The comprehensive portion of my auto insurance increased 300 percent.

At that time Mississippi was proclaiming that because

of its stable society and the mutual understanding and respect between races it had no record of vandalism such as the rest of the country was experiencing. Our area in Kentucky had been known locally for some such problems. Yet when I inquired of my insurance agent why the increase in comprehensive rates, he replied that it was set by the state insurance commission, and that the given reason was the high incidence of vandalism. Actually, my car did suffer from vandalism — someone put long scratches as with a knife blade on each door — while parked on a Jackson street within a couple of blocks of the governor's mansion, though how common such incidents were I have no idea. Perhaps vandalism was rampant, and it was the other side of its mouth out of which the state was lying; or perhaps there was little vandalism outside the commission which set insurance rates.

In any case, living was not cheaper in Mississippi; not even housing was cheaper, though we moved to an area of much unused land from the old, settled, extremely valuable Blue Grass country.

Louisiana is in part a different story. It has the lowest telephone rates I have encountered, and they still have, or did when I lived there from 1961 to 1963, nickel pay phones. This, a friend told me, was a result of the Huey Long philosophy that no monopoly would be allowed to exploit the people of Louisiana but his own. Partly or principally because of Long, Louisiana costs less to live in generally than any place I have been; the $3 car tags alone saved about $40 a year of the ad valorem tax I would have paid in Mississippi.

Lacking benevolent dictators as its heritage, Mississippi is low in wages and in purchasing power, and that largely because of the racial situation. With the Negro always

available and hungry, and available and hungry because
as a Negro he has little chance to advance, it is easy to
keep all wages down, so long as unions are kept away.
The same forces, such as the Jackson newspapers, which
foster segregation the hardest also fight the unions hardest. One reason is evident in the fact that a few years ago
a proofreader of my acquaintance left a Jackson paper for
a (union) Memphis paper and drew twice as much money
for the same job. From all accounts, the Jackson paper
was in quite as good financial condition as the Memphis
paper, perhaps better.

While my wife was working during the summer of 1959,
we hired a Negro high school girl to do housework, cook,
and look after the children. The going rate for experienced help was $12 a week. We paid her, apologetically,
$60 a month. There were good reasons for paying no
more, completely aside from the fact that by the time
my wife had paid social security, taxes, transportation and
incidental expenses, and the girl, the residue was scarcely
worth the bother. If you paid too much above the going
rate, you were likely to bring the general white populace
down not only upon yourself, but upon the girl and her
family, too.

Her pay, moreover, was within a very few dollars of the
rate an excellent cleaning woman at the college had
worked up to in twenty years.

I have often wondered why the white man, who knows
that his own employers will deliberately keep the Negro
subservient in order to exploit him financially, does not
consider that he himself is subject to the same process.
At the school where the cleaning woman worked, salaries
were not startlingly high for the white people, and of
course the same sorts of evasion were used on us as were
used on the Negroes.

I recall a fund-raising drive during which we teachers were told that faculty salaries was the chief aim — and we should all support the drive so that at the kickoff dinner alumni and friends could be informed the faculty was 100 percent behind it. The professional fund raiser suggested that he would like to be able to announce that the (small) faculty had pledged, say $25,000. One of the ladies raised her hand. "If we gave that much," she said, "wouldn't they ask why we need our salaries increased?"

The man's mouth fell open beneath his sincere blue eyes and he stammered the beginnings of several abortive sentences. Finally he said, "We'd answer something." Of course, he did not have to answer anything, lacking $25,000 and 100 percent support. And anyway, the printed goals for the campaign listed faculty salaries seventh.

The segregationist argument that Mississippi gains economically by virtue of its "way of life" is nonsense. It should be evident that raising half the populace from tax burdens to consumers would be a tremendous boost to the economy, but the Negro is not allowed to rise, no matter how "separate but equal" people talk. Even outside the South, as Robert Moses, a leading civil rights worker in Mississippi, has pointed out, those people who try to solve the Negro's problem often approach it on the basis of "if it were not for existing difficulties, then . . ." He says that he has sat in on meetings for discussion of the Negro's economic plight, at which the decision is that his economy cannot be improved until he has a better education. Then he has sat in on school meetings where it is decided that nothing can be done until the housing problem is solved so that zoning does not put the Negro always into a segregated, inferior school. Then he has sat in on housing meetings which conclude that nothing

can be done until the Negro's economic situation is improved and he can afford the houses in better neighbor-
hoods. Those are the people who try.

In Mississippi the established effort is in the other
direction. I am appalled whenever I hear a fellow Mississippian repeating as gospel the concepts of race, religion,
and economy he has been taught consistently by particular people who sit behind the scenes and, to my personal
knowledge, control an extremely large amount of the
news and opinion allowed to be circulated in Mississippi,
certain very important political figures, and a vast area
of the state's financial situation. The working Mississippian directly, and the professional Mississippian more
nearly indirectly, have by these same people been literally
robbed of both economic opportunity and the opportunity
to know what is going on in the state and in the world,
of both money itself and voice in the government, of both
a sound economic system and the chance to live on a
decent basis with their fellowmen and fellow citizens.
Yet, caught by the economy, by propaganda, by law, and
by fear — all perceptibly operated by these same few
people — the Mississippian has convinced himself that
their doctrines are God's truth and that their way of life
is the road to glory. Slavery didn't end in Mississippi with
Emancipation; it merely began insidiously including white
people.

Some elements of the economic situation in Mississippi
have begun to come into the open. It is doubtful that
many Mississippians will read Jim Silver's *Mississippi:
The Closed Society,* where the problem is dealt with intel-
ligently and factually, and it is likely that those who do
will largely discount it; Silver has been the target of lies
and vituperation for years because of his refusal to falsify
along with the bosses and their frightened little negative

yes-men. But things do break through now and then.

Recently Murray W. Latimer, head of a Washington, D. C., firm of industrial relations consultants, returned to his home town to dedicate a new business building, for which his family gave the land, at Mississippi College. I hear that he made an excellent speech and that many people received it well, although I also read in the local paper a long diatribe against him by the gossip columnist. Since then the Mississippi College *Beacon* has published a valuable, though abbreviated, account of Latimer's speech, which he based on a four-month study of the state, and some results of a further study by the college's business department head, Dr. Gray Miley. The article appropriately features the quotation from II Corinthians 10:12, ". . . but they, measuring themselves among themselves, and comparing themselves among themselves, are not wise."

Briefly, Dr. Miley's research indicates that at the present rate of gain Mississippi should reach the national average of personal income in 360 years. Latimer sees the present rate as somewhat better, but expects it to be retarded because of a number of economic factors, including Mississippi's hostility to trade unions. Another factor is listed in these words:

> The "division of Mississippi's economy into two distinct and largely non-homogenous parts — white and Negro — provides a host of unfortunate economic repercussions." Among them: half the State's population provides deficient local markets for Mississippi products. . . .

The tone of both Latimer's and Miley's remarks is that the state is fooling itself about its economy and had better wake up to facts.

The only real economic advantage I have been able to discover in segregation is immediate and limited — it has increased the quick profits of those who need money least, and that at the cost of retarding, together, the profiteer's own business and the whole economy. And at the cost of no telling how much misery for those deprived of an adequate living and of hope for any way out.

XVIII

Past Confusions
and Present Fears

THE ABSTRACT TAPESTRY of Southern and quasi-Southern
political thought is confused in part by two dominant and
distinct colors of the past.

The gray and guilty past: If it had not been for New
England slavers, if it had not been for abolitionists, if it
had not been for the industrialization of the North, if it
had not been for Reconstruction, we would have no
troubles today.

The golden past: If it were not for today's do-gooders,
socialists, integrationists, Communists, and the federal
government, who are destroying the sweet order and
clean simplicity that used to be, what a fine world we
would be living in!

The two ideas often exist in the same head, and they
provide a handy device for argument — the man with
alternate pasts can switch grounds at the turn of a ques-

tion. It seems never to occur to him that the sweet order
had its slave trade which led to disorder, nor does he ever
argue that it is the do-gooders who helped destroy the
slave trade which was so evil. Right-hand pocket, the
past was evil and to blame for our present ills; left-hand
pocket, the past was perfect; and in our hearts we know
both are, separately, true.

The principle is not limited, however, to the Southern
mind. I have heard Northern do-gooders argue that the
Negro is not to blame for his lack of knowledge, skill, am-
bition, or what have you: it is his cultural background
that is to blame, and said background is the product of
the Southern white man. The Southern white man, however, has no excuse. *His* cultural background has nothing
to do with it. And beneath the Yankee accent we discover
a familiar Southern tune — the superiority of the white
man, who is human and responsible, over the black man,
who is really not quite human and so not responsible. It
is just as possible to be integrationistically as segregation-
istically illogical and patronizing.

Some while back a very bright and disillusioned young
Negro revealed a few continuing illusions about "culture."
He blamed white people for not accepting the Negro
without any effort. To be right and acceptable the white
man had, not to overcome, but to obliterate his cultural
background. The Negro, on the other hand, was said to
be in a nearly hopeless condition, as compared to the
white man, because he had no culture. I offered the
young man my own culture, that of white Mississippi, in
exchange for his. He didn't swap, but then I suppose that
neither of us knew how, and I really didn't want to anyway.

The problem of the historical past, the cultural past, the

individual past is extremely complex, but we often make it more difficult to comprehend than necessary by confusing it with popular psychology as a means of excusing ourselves and laying the blame on others.

The same is true of property rights and states' rights, the two prime legalisms that underlie the Southern excuse for segregation. Time and again I have been told that a man should have absolute freedom to do what he wants to with his property, and told it (in buildings erected on zoned land according to building codes) by people who so strongly object to the thought of some young man's running his privately owned mobile property over a spot on which they happen to be standing that they loudly advocate local, state, and federal laws against teen-age drivers. Of course private property is a right, but only one of many rights, none of which in this world can be absolute. Jefferson even forgot to mention it when, in the Declaration of Independence, he limited himself for rhetorical balance to three elemental rights back when everything was orderly and clear if you were not there fighting your friends and countrymen.

To states' rights advocates, not only does the "or to the people" phrase dim out of the Tenth Amendment, but the reasons for hating and fearing a strong centralized federal government vanish when strong centralized state governments are considered. In Mississippi local government advocates have given the governor an enlarged Highway Patrol and power to send it as a police force into any county or city without invitation and against the will of the local authorities and local populace.

The federal government is to be feared because it is bureaucratic and threatens to take away our rights, Mississippians say. The Republican candidate for governor in 1963 was reported as producing evidence that Mississippi has more employees and more agencies per capita than does the federal government.

Anyone in Mississippi preoccupied with fear of the federal government's taking away his rights is like a man so concerned about the matches in the pocket of the hired man in the barn that he instinctively withdraws further into his burning house.

My students used constantly to declare that "the federal government has taken away all of our rights."

Eventually I began to ask, "Which rights? Name one right the federal government has taken away from you."

Blank faces. Absolutely blank. A boy did once reply that the government was taking away his right to go to a school without such people as James Meredith. I tried to point out the difference in the white person's being free either to go to Ole Miss or to stay away from it, whereas Meredith had been, by the state government, forced to stay away. The federal government — quite conceivably capable of taking away rights too — was merely removing illegal force against a citizen who had as much right as any other citizen to attend the school his taxes were supporting. And further, no citizen had the right, anyway, arbitrarily to exclude his fellow citizens from a public school; the government could not take away a right which was not a right to begin with.

The students could think of no specifics, but they knew, as we all generally do, that their position was nevertheless sound, and that if they could just get the facts they could prove it.

"All right," I said finally, "if you want to discover which government it is you're really afraid of, try it out. Go down to the courthouse square, get a crowd, and begin berating the President, the nine old Communist judges of the Supreme Court, the policies of Congress. Say anything disparaging you can think of, especially against integration."

They listened, wondering but unmoved. They had heard such speeches before.

"Then," I said, "go to the opposite side of the square, and stand up and say aloud that you believe segregation is wrong and that you believe the United States Supreme Court ruling must be enforced."

There was no need to go further. The students still sat without moving, but their faces turned very pale.

XIX

Children of God

THE SOUTH IS, as I have said, very religious, and it equates religion with Christianity and Christianity, all too often, with the doctrine that the white people of the South are God's chosen people. Earlier I tried to indicate a difference between Christian religion and Christianity. The South believes strongly in God and the Bible, believes itself to be Christian, and then ignores, as a body, the basic teachings of Christ. It preaches that at salvation the nature of man is changed to the nature of God, which is love, and then it operates churches on the opposite principle.

Of course, not all Southerners are this way, and too often Chrisitans who expect too much of other Christians forget both that they are supposed, themselves, to be loving and forgiving and that when Jesus spoke of the many who would go down the road to destruction and the few who would enter by the strait and narrow gate, when He spoke of wolves in sheep's clothing, and when He spoke of those who cry, "Lord, Lord," He was obviously talking about the body of the religious. Few there be, in any religion or out.

Baptists in the South rate condemnation from their fellow Christians of the rest of the country who fail to see the identical spirit in the ecumenical council when it seriously discusses whether to be anti-Semitic for yet another century or so because according to God's plan Jesus was crucified by the most available human beings, his fellow Jews. And when it is argued by some Cardinals that, regardless of the rightness of removing accusation from the Jews now living, to make such a stand public would cause trouble in Arabic countries, one hears the echo of the Southern ministry that we mustn't cause dissension and maybe split the Church.

Once I heard a Baptist minister remark that nowadays they don't feed a preacher to the lions if he preaches the truth — they just don't feed him. In the few years since he said that, of course, some arenas have been under construction.

It is not my purpose to castigate Christians or to point out their inconsistencies except as they affect other people; however much belief is private, action is public, and the preaching of diabolical doctrines as coming from God needs to be countered socially to the extent that they excuse and encourage social injustice. A man is welcome to his religion as long as he does not sacrifice other folk at the altar.

It seems fruitless to argue with those people, and they do exist in some abundance, who delve into the Book of Daniel and come up with a variety of esoteric self-justifi-

cations. Where there is runic superstition, reason has no
effect; anyway such peculiar doctrines are heard only by
the already convinced. But other Southern and non-
Southern concepts of Christianity are preached which
solidly bolster cowardice and inhumanity. According to
one such interpretation the Golden Rule means that if I
don't want to sit with a Negro, he should not sit with me,
rather than since I don't want people to be rude to me,
I should not be rude to them, and I must give to the
other man any rights I myself desire. The saying has even
been twisted into a bargain: Okay, I won't treat you decently and you don't have to treat me decently.

Love thy neighbor as thyself, becomes claim to treat
each individual well, but persecute the race. People vote
for segregation, then lay the blame on the law. Render
unto Caesar, they say, the things that are Caesar's; law
is Caesar's. They forget that it was tax money Jesus spoke
of, and further that in a democracy we are Caesar. We
make the law. A citizen in a democracy who votes for,
fails to vote against, or supports the promulgators of a
law which deals unjustly with his fellowman is just as
guilty as was Nero for laws against the early Christians.

It is fascinating to watch with what glee certain people
have latched onto the phrase, "You can't legislate morality." Of course most of the laws it is used against attempt
neither to legislate morality nor to legislate against immorality, but to legislate against crime. We might as well
say, no use passing a law against picking pockets since
you can't make a thief honest by passing a law: you can't
legislate morality. You can't make a murderer love people
by passing a law.

Of course not. But you can make a law against a man's
stealing my money, and against a man's taking my life.

You can make a law against a man's taking my rights —
and we have been doing so all along.

No use, I have wanted to reply, trying to make a Negro
good by passing a segregation law. If he wants to be bad
and try to integrate, you can't make him good by law.
You can't legislate morality.

It is especially interesting to hear the phrase in Jackson,
say, with its Sunday "Blue Laws," or anywhere coupled
with anger at the Supreme Court for having driven God
out of the United States. Unfortunately, the phrase is
nationwide, as too much of the country gathers headlong
momentum down the road paved with such good intentions to Mississippi-ism.

Recently in the Mississippi *Baptist Record* a minister
replied to charges of non-Southern preachers that the
ministry in the South was shirking its duty by ignoring
the racial situation. The minister said that, first, they had
not ignored it. They have preached on love all along.
Second, many preachers genuinely believe in separation
of church and state, and they do not believe in using the
pulpit to meddle in political matters.

A few, perhaps. I assume, though I am not positive,
that Southern Baptists still have a paid lobbyist in Washington. I know they did a few years ago. I know further
that I have heard minister after minister preach against
not just liquor but the legalization of liquor as a specifically political issue. I have heard preachers castigate
John F. Kennedy, strike out at socialism, and advocate
segregation from the pulpit. One minister used the dance
called the Twist as a catchy lead into an article in his
church bulletin, and casually remarked that he did not
like the Twist and if it were in his power he would
eradicate it.

I'm afraid most of those who "cannot legislate morality" are like some of his fellow ministers who, my father
has said privately, are Baptists only because they knew
they could never make Pope. They would if they could.

Another religious dodge has to do with the Sermon on
the Mount as a fine document but not applicable in practice, since Jesus was talking about an ideal world, the
world the way it would be if everybody were Christian —
and so the Christian now may act as if everybody including himself is un-Christian. But if everyone were perfect,
who would slap the first cheek so that you could turn the
other? Where would this evil come from that is sufficient
unto the day? And what enemies would there be to love?

It is all right to be Christian and wrong, but all wrong
to be non-Christian and right, to a great many segregationists. Witness a meeting of the ruling body of a Mississippi church over the problem of what to do if Negroes
should appear at the church door. After some maneuver-
ings to avoid the issue, and others to set it up so that
"integrationists" would be out in the open and subject to
intimidation or at least to the feeling that they would
be targets of reprisals, the body held its discussion. The
minister, a Mississippian, preached a brief sermon saying
that Christians should never deny admittance to anybody
who desired to attend church, and that a visitor's motivation should not be judged — even if he were a troublemaker, the best method would be to seat him quietly and
avoid demonstrations and television cameras on the
church steps.

Several men spoke up to say the time was not right.
One spoke of force being used in the state, another said
that the rule might be all right for the North or the East,
but the South could never change its traditions, and one

said that although we might feel sorry for the Negroes, bringing them into the church was the wrong thing. There was a statement that the work of the "motley crew" of summer integrationists was certainly un-Christian, and another man added that the local law officers should be called if a Negro appeared, because anybody knows the motivation of Negroes who come to a white church when they have just as good churches of their own.

These men were successful business and professional men, some with advanced degrees and important positions in the community and the state. Nearly everyone who spoke against the minister's stand began with a statement like, "I know I'm not as good a Christian as I should be and that I don't know as much about the Bible and theology as the preacher does, but . . ." Some admitted that the preacher was probably right, but then would virtually beg that their way of life not be changed.

One, a football coach, stood up nervously, with tears in his eyes, and made his plea: "The preacher and I have talked about this thing lots of times. Now, he says what he thinks is right. Well, I *know* what is right. I admit that I have not been as good a Christian as I should have been. I will admit that I *need* the church. But the church just cannot help me if it is going to let the colored people and troublemakers start coming to church."

They used to ask us to imagine, when I was a boy in Sunday school, what it would be like if Jesus came into the world today.

XX

Born into the World

IN RECENT YEARS the word "rights" has been in every-body's vocabulary, often preceded by such qualifications as "civil," "constitutional," or "God-given." No matter what the label, however, the meanings run from pole to pole. Of either legal or "God-given" rights, it is good to recall that the letter killeth, but the spirit giveth life. Injustice can be justified by manipulations of legal texts, even the Constitution, and by scriptural authority, but the basic constitutional spirit of the equality of rights and privileges of all citizens and the basic religious spirit of love are hard put to inspire injustice, except for that form of injustice we call mercy.

Many individual laws and situations are involved in genuine complexities, of course, but on the other hand deliberate complexity on a simple issue is also common. It seems to me necessary that we constantly check ourselves with the simple question: Am I actually operating on the basis of a free offering to every man of what I expect myself?

Rights may be understood more clearly without the theological and doctrinal intricacies associated in too many minds with "God-given," and without the legal questions involved in the minds of many when the Constitution is invoked. Basic rights are easily illustrated. We human beings are all here in the same boat, and the only way we can work out a reasonably satisfactory arrangement is by a necessary species of agreement: by virtue of being here, each person has the same rights and responsibilities. If I shove one man out, I must expect to be shoved out in turn. If we agree that there is to be no shoving out, however, then we can operate together and get some sleep too. The one who does shove is shoved back into place by the group for having violated the other man's right to be left unshoved. It is not necessary for the offended man, if he survives, to fight back alone, or for the shover to be allowed to keep shoving people overboard so long as he's successful. The basic right is: to be treated as of equal value — not shoved.

The concept is extended when it comes to passing the drinking water. We cannot afford to refuse to pass it to the bow, because then the bow will have precedent, when we go to sleep and they capture the water, not to pass it to us. If we are to live, we must cooperate, and that not just in our little corner.

Obviously, mankind has never learned the lesson, but it is still necessary to act upon the basis of such rights if we're to do as well as possible. Doing so is what we call good, doing otherwise is what we call bad.

The whole idea, I have no doubt, will be dismissed as

in language like a primer and in concept like a platitude. And so it is. Its critics may love or hate with their own intricate sophistications if they choose — the childish concept is true and basic. The whole of morality, however complex the superstructure, and the whole of human relationships, in fact and in the convoluted studies of Henry James, rest on this foundation.

One former Southerner told me that he left years ago partly because it bothered him that his friends treated Negroes as if they were not human. That is a simple concept, but I know many clever men who lead distorted lives because they have never learned to honor it.

I have offered no solution, because although I, too, believe that if everybody would just do right everything humanly controlled would be fine, and although much of the right seems to me to be obvious, I know that most of us do right only if it won't hurt us. And further, a great many well-meaning people have never, through lack of intelligence, training, courage, and a complex of other lacks, gone to the basis of anything to understand the spirit and purpose of it.

I used to see a tall, thin, khaki-clad man walking the sidewalks near the courthouse square, one place we lived. He would stride along with measured steps, his face straight ahead, his eye on the traffic light. When the light turned red, he stopped dead still, ostentatiously, and when the light turned green he set off again, obviously pleased with his accomplishment. The saddest part was that he stopped in mid-block as well as at cross streets.

A well-known evangelist came through when I was about twelve, and I sat through one of his sermons. The man spoke about God with great conviction, but he said absolutely nothing. He seemed, in fact, to use all his considerable talents to avoid saying anything. When the sermon was over a very fine lady sitting near me exclaimed, "Wasn't that a wonderful sermon!"

"God" equals go. "Devil" equals stop. Then the forces, the people, controlling news, religion, and politics, change the signs gradually until "God" equals white and "Devil" equals black; and white equals us, black equals them; us equals Americans, them equals Communists. Go. Stop. Go. Stop. And never look to see whether there is even an intersection underfoot.

It has always been pretty much that way. I heard an excerpt from a recent Columbus Day speech which implied that our age is degenerate because we lack the spirit of Columbus, as if the whole world and not Columbus almost alone had that spirit, as if the body of our Puritan forebears were believers in freedom instead of Quaker-hangers, as if the Confederacy were the noblest aspects of Stonewall Jackson and Robert E. Lee instead of men who essentially put their own economic well-being above human life and value, as if Abraham Lincoln were not one of the most caricatured and vilified of Presidents by his own Union.

What I cherish in our past and in our age is not so much the generality — the greed and fear and superstition — but the line of intelligence and responsibility and courage and love that has come down through all our great men at their best, and through their critics and opponents at their best, and through the Puritans and the plantation owners at their respective best. It has added up to a great deal, and it has immense possibilities even now.

It seems that every Southerner who writes critically about the South is supposed to say at some point that he loves the South. William Faulkner has been reported as saying that we love, not because of, but in spite of; and unquestionably I do care what happens to and in the South, and I love many of its people without honoring elements of its past any more than I do its often unlovely present. Faulkner's critics often call attention, too, to the statement by Quentin Compson in *Absalom, Absalom!* that you have to be born in the South to understand. But being born in the world is essentially the same thing — just as incomprehensible and unreasonable and unreal, so that the human condition is that, having known nothing else, we nevertheless find life strange.